Some Approaches to Research in Music Education

CONTENTS

CONTRIBUTORS

Clem Adelman is Professor of Education in the Department of Education Studies and Management at the University of Reading, England.

Harold Fiske is Professor of Music in the Faculty of Music at the University of Western Ontario, London, Canada.

Anthony Kemp is Senior Lecturer and Head of the Department of Arts and Humanities at the University of Reading, England.

Laurence Lepherd is Associate Professor and Associate Dean in the School of Arts at the University of Southern Queensland, Australia.

Bernarr Rainbow was formerly Head of Music at Kingston Polytechnic, England and was one of the first to identify and record the social history of music.

Cornelia Yarbrough is Professor of Music and Coordinator of Music Education at Louisiana State University, Baton Rouge, USA.

Some Approaches to Research in Music Education

Edited by

ANTHONY E. KEMP

ISME Edition Number Five

Published by International Society for Music Education
ISME International Office
University of Reading
Bulmershe Court
READING RG6 1HY
England.
ISBN 1 871015 01 4
Printed by The Charlesworth Group, Huddersfield, England, 0484 517077

Preface

During the period 1988 to 1990 the Research Commission of the International Society of Music Education took the conscious decision to develop a more lively role in encouraging the wider ISME membership to be more research minded. The Commission took the view that, at whatever level music teachers teach, or whatever form their work takes, a research attitude was likely to enhance their professional performance as teachers. It was felt that nothing was to be gained by shrouding the work of the researcher in an aura of mysticism which exacerbated the gulf between the researcher and teacher and which had tended to exist for far too long.

A second resolve of the Commission related to the notion that it should adopt a wider view of what constitutes research, broadening out the range to encourage more philosophical, historical, comparative and other forms of qualitative research in addition to the experimental work for which the Commission had largely made its reputation.

It was therefore decided that the Commission should arrange a series of presentations at the ISME World Conference in Helsinki in August 1990 focusing on research approaches and methods for those delegates who were interested in undertaking research perhaps for the first time. Six presentations were organized as a part of the Conference programme along with the Commission's first poster session. These sessions were packed by large numbers of delegates, in fact several were overcrowded, indicating the extent of the need for this kind of information and expertise felt amongst delegates from all over the world.

This volume by and large represents the papers delivered at the Helsinki Conference and is designed to support all those who wish to take a more inquiring attitude towards their everyday work as music educators. As Chairman of the Commission throughout this period I wish to thank its other members, Harold Fiske, Ana Lucia Frega, Janina Fyk, Clifford Madsen and Bertil Sundin for their invaluable support in seeing these ideas through to fruition.

In addition, I wish to express my gratitude to several colleagues in the Faculty of Education and Community Studies at the University of Reading, namely, John Gilbert, Keith Watson, Clem Adelman, Brian Richards and Gordon Cox as well as my former colleague, Arnold Bentley, for reading some of the chapters. Their helpful criticism and comments were much appreciated and any weaknesses which remain should be seen as my responsibility alone.

University of Reading   Anthony Kemp
June 1992

1

Approaching Research

ANTHONY E. KEMP

Education is not a unitary discipline. Traditionally, the study of education has led its students quite naturally into the fields of philosophy, psychology and sociology and, in addition, they may also seek enlightenment from the anthropologist, the historian and the comparativist. Music educationists frequently become involved in an even wider canvas simply because the study of music also possesses its own cluster of disciplines. Some of these music shares with education, such as history and sociology and, more occasionally, perhaps psychology and anthropology, but more central to its own concerns lie the study of music's literature, techniques and styles of performance and composition, frequently involving skill acquisition, analysis, interpretation and criticism. Occasionally, students of music may also wish to pursue areas within aesthetics. Research in music education may therefore find itself operating within a combination of two or more disciplines which feature in the two groups mentioned above. Perhaps the most comprehensive picture of the complexity of the field can be gained by glancing through the *Handbook of Research on Music Teaching and Learning* (Colwell, 1992) which devotes 55 chapters to the various aspects of music education research. Given such a complex map of what may constitute research in music education, where, and at what point does the initiate start?

All research starts with identifying a problem. The kinds of problem addressed by researchers are those which arise, not out of the researcher's ignorance, but from a firm knowledge of both the particular context of the problem as well as the literature which relates to it. Thus, the first lesson to be learned by the person contemplating research is that significant experience in the field as well as a firm knowledge of the literature are very necessary prerequisites to making any decision concerning a research problem. In practice, the processes of reviewing the literature and formulating a statement of the problem are interactive; the more the researcher engages in analytical reading the more he or she will want to modify and clarify the research area. On the other hand, as the area becomes clearer so do the boundaries of the supporting literature become more defined. The point cannot be made too forcefully that data collection, whatever form it may take, should not commence until this preliminary work has been completed.

Reviewing the literature helps to prevent a re-invention of the wheel and discovering that similar work has been successfully completed already. However, it should be pointed out that there is an inevitable time-lag between the identification of issues which require researchers' attention and the outcomes of research relating to these issues appearing in the literature. Hopefully persons contemplating research will be mindful of the burning questions occurring within their work context and will be knowledgeable about the kinds of issues which need addressing. In addition, it is also important that a research question is selected which the researcher finds both interesting and absorbing.

Research in music education is particularly characterized by a profusion of one-off research studies which all too frequently fail to relate to each other in any real coherent way. Two points need to be made in this connection: firstly, that an effective and conscientious reviewing of the international literature enables the researcher to engage in work which relates effectively to the field in question, and secondly, that there is a pronounced need within music education for more studies, if not to replicate earlier inquiries, to approach similar problems in different ways. For a few examples of research which exemplify a clarity of purpose and reflect admirable coherence, the reader is encouraged to turn to Fry (1988); Davies, Kenny and Barbenel (1989); Sloboda (1991); Sloboda and Howe (1991).

The search for relevant material to review will concentrate on library facilities. Each library may be differently organized but will normally have card index systems and computerized retrieval facilities. The card indices will allow the reader to identify books of a specialist or general nature which will be useful to help in becoming familiar with the field. They may also identify a number of additional and important references. There will also be a listing of the journals and periodicals held in the library; this will require studying to discover which journals are likely to relate to the reader's research interests. Clearly some libraries are better stocked than others and it is essential that links are forged, wherever possible, with a major library which specializes in music education. Journals can be searched 'by hand' but this is slow and laborious, and, if possible, use should be made of one or more of the computer data bases available. Some of these relate directly to music such as *Repertoires International de Literature Musicale, Music Index* and *Music Psychology*

Index. More general educational indices which may help in identifying relevant material are *Educational Resources Information Center* (the ERIC system), *Dissertation Abstracts International, Music Literature International (RILM), British Education Index, Arts and Humanities Search* and, if appropriate, *Psychological Abstracts.* If access is available to a university library there may well be collections of theses amongst which relevant material may be found particularly if that university has a music education department with an active research group. Theses completed in other universities are listed in *Dissertation Abstracts International*, and most of these will be available on microfilm.

It is generally advisable to pursue the most recent material first. This will offer the most up-to-date reviews and some of the most recent references. By locating these additional references and working backwards, a feeling for how the work in the area has developed will be gained. A knowledge of the principal researchers in the field will also be developed and, at a later stage, correspondence may be developed with them. The process of gathering the relevant literature together is likely to be near completion when a current issue of a respected reviewed journal contains an article directly within the field which contains the bulk of material which has already been located.

Throughout the whole process of searching the literature be sure that well organized notes are kept which may take the form of a card index or computer data files. Whatever form the notes take, be meticulous about recording names and initials of authors, exact titles and dates of publication. If the publication is an article, the name of the journal, volume number and page numbers should be noted; if it is a book note its edition, place of publication and name of publisher. These notes will become the basis of your list of references or bibliography when, later, the research report will require writing.

Notes can be organized in several different ways, either on the backs of the cards in a card index, or by developing files which relate to various aspects of the research problem. However, computer-based systems are increasingly being used by researchers, allowing information to be stored in such a fashion that it can be retrieved simply and in a form which may make the process of writing up the research at the end much less cumbersome. Notes, whatever form they take, should contain page numbers for particular and important points and observations in books, journals and theses. This is particularly important in those instances where a note is being made of a passage which, later, may be required as a quotation. Nothing is more irritating at the writing up stage than having significant quotations to hand without adequate details of their location, necessitating a new and often laborious search.

A very necessary aspect of this preliminary work may involve narrowing down the focus of the proposed research. Once placed under close scrutiny, research questions have a habit of splitting into series of sub-questions, frequently inviting the researcher to narrow down the focus by selecting one of these. If this occurs a student may, unwisely, neglect the opportunity to select one element and, at a later stage, may find that the research area has become hopelessly unmanageable and unfocused as a result. Some research students find that the process of searching the literature may have the effect of unfocusing and broadening their topics. This occurs when a student becomes side-tracked into a related area which he or she finds absorbing but which has only a tenuous link with the proposed research. In such instances the student needs to keep the original intentions and boundaries of the research topic in mind.

It did not happen by accident that, in several countries of the world, research degrees are designated as being in philosophy. It can be maintained that, in a sense, all research should be in philosophy in that it is through philosophical discourse that we learn to conceptualize, define terms, maintain valid arguments, establish causal relationships and arrive at conclusions with a fair degree of confidence. At the point of formulating a research question, adopting a philosophical stance is particularly important. As mentioned earlier, an apparently simple question, after a degree of reflection and analysis, may emerge as a complex cluster of issues each of which may warrant its own inquiry. In the early stages of planning research, philosophical analysis will therefore help prevent the researcher from pursuing an unanalysed question which would inevitably lead to unfocused research and, in turn, to the gathering of data which might become unmanageable. Also, within the field of music education countless terms are commonly used like 'creativity', 'musicianship', 'aesthetic experience', 'music appreciation' yet may serve to prevent accurate communication or sharp thinking because they represent clusters of different shades of meaning according to the background of their users. The problem becomes even more pronounced at international research gatherings where language difficulties may occur anyway without additional misunderstandings arising out of undefined terms taking on different meanings in different cultural contexts. Taking up a philosophical stance by asking the question 'what do you mean by this or that term?' helps the researcher to clarify a research question to the point where it can be conceived as being a workable or testable hypothesis.

The focus of the research must be specific. Titles such as 'musical performance in primary schools' or 'rock music in the secondary school curriculum' require reducing into specific questions. More acceptable questions might relate to 'the relationship between scores on a rhythmic performance test and pupils' age in an infant school' or 'what musical concepts and skills required by the National Curriculum at age 14 can be effectively taught through the use of rock music?' Clearly the experimental researcher will be required to frame these kind of questions into specific hypotheses; the action researcher, on the other hand, will need to decide on what form his or her intervention should most appropriately take.

Good research arises out of good research questions. Good questions will have not only been analysed to eliminate undue complexity and inexact language but should also be assessed as to the degree of relevance that they have, either to the processes of contemporary education or to the research community. Research questions should also be researchable, that is, answerable through the processes and strategies used within the various methodologies. Research questions then, can be classified into specific types, each relating to a methodology which tends to prescribe the nature of the (a) evidence being collected (b) method of its collection (c) method of analysing the evidence (d) style of presenting the evidence. It is important to be clear in one's mind about the purpose of the research: to whom are the results to be addressed? Who needs to be convinced? What kind of evidence is likely to convince them? For example, it is clear that teachers will heed a very different form of evidence from, say, governments or politicians. Wierzma (1986), Cohen and Manion (1989) amongst several others have described the variety of research methods generally adopted by educational researchers; similar and very comprehensive reviews of research methods in music education can be found in Rainbow and Froehlich (1987) and Colwell (1992).

We have set out here to introduce the reader to the essential features of a selected number of methodologies. Each contributor has been asked, firstly to describe the type of research question which their methodology is best able to address, and secondly, to introduce the reader to the types of research design and techniques which are adopted to approach these questions. Whilst working within these two remits each author has been asked to refer to a number of selected exemplars of published research within the field.

One way of viewing the various methodologies selected for inclusion in this book is to focus on the degree of distancing of the researcher from the actual objects of the respective research approaches. In historical research, the most distanced from 'reality', the researcher is required to construct accurate accounts of conditions, issues and trends which have occurred in the past through the analysis and evaluation of primary and secondary sources of information. In this work, the historian, normally totally excluded and distanced from the era in question, attempts to become transported back in time through a synthesis of the various perspectives of past observers and commentators. The reader is encouraged to take a look at Rainbow (1970) for an admirable example of the past coming to life through the process of synthesizing information from historical documents.

Unlike the historian, the comparativist normally operates within his or her own time frame and may frequently have some first hand experience of the situations being reviewed or compared. In comparative research the data relate to methods, strategies and issues adopted by nations or, alternatively, social groups or institutions within nations. Comparativists, like historians, are required to make considerable efforts to develop insights and a rapport with the particular focus of their research especially when this lies outside their own cultural background. The reader will draw considerable insights into this particular process from chapter three where Laurence Lepherd discusses the ways in which he was able to develop a familiarity with Chinese and Russian contexts.

The experimental researcher may, or may not, have direct contact with the subjects of the research. Through the process of manipulation, the researcher controls and alters the factors under investigation. By controlling one variable (independent variable) the researcher is able to assess the influence this has exercised on a second variable (dependent variable). Regardless of the kind of experimental group design adopted, the investigator may choose to remain remote simply because the focus of the study relates less to the first-hand knowledge of the research subjects than to the data being assembled. An objective distancing by the researcher, whether present or absent, is necessary in order to prevent any contamination of the data being collected. This objectivity is inevitably reflected in the style of reporting which will be discussed in the final chapter. Many examples of research which take this kind of stance towards the researched can be found, particularly in such journals as *Psychology of Music*, *Journal of Research in Music Education*, and the *Bulletin of the Council for Research in Music Education*.

In observational research the investigator is not only present, but is actively present. Whether the researcher adopts a naturalistic or an experimental approach, the focus of the research relates to the actual behaviour patterns of the subjects in responding to well defined tasks within carefully controlled conditions over particular periods of time. Cornelia Yarbrough's chapter clearly takes an experimental stance towards observational research and, within these kinds of conditions, the investigator is required to record in a systematic way the behavioural responses to the stimuli under investigation.

Finally, case studies and action research are carried out in the real world of the classroom or studio. In both approaches the researcher may be fully engaged in the activity under investigation and, in this sense they can be said to be self-evaluative. The essential characteristic of action research is that it encourages teachers to become teacher-researchers and, unlike case studies, involves a clearly identifiable form of intervention. The action researcher is enabled to develop strategies to solve his or her own pedagogical problems. Adelman and Kemp have done their best in identifying research which, it is hoped, the reader will find both illuminating and helpful.

The last chapter of the book is designed to provide the reader with some general guidelines which relate to writing research reports. Clearly, these guidelines can only be general, for there are several differences between the methodologies represented in this book and space does not allow for these to be explored any more fully. Besides providing this essential advice, the chapter also serves to remind the reader that many a strong piece of research has been marred by incomplete, verbose or poorly structured reporting.

One sometimes hears the complaint from music teachers that many forms of research in music education are too complex to be either intelligible or of practical relevance to music in the classroom or studio. They maintain that, all too often, researchers unnecessarily overcomplicate the various processes of music learning and teaching which they choose to investigate. It is the general view of the authors contributing to this book that these processes are indeed very often complex but that a fully competent teacher will wish to possess these insights as a part of their professional development. Those teachers who are heard to make such complaints may well lack a grasp of the full complexity of the work in which they are engaging.

References

Berkshire Local Education Authority (1989). *Classroom Issues in Assessment and Evaluation in the Arts*. Reading: Berkshire Local Education Authority.

Cohen, L. and Manion, L. (1989). *Research Methods in Education* (3rd edn.). London: Routledge.

Colwell, R. (ed.) (1992). *Handbook for Research in Music Teaching and Learning*. New York: Schirmer.

Davies, C. (1992). Listen to my Song: A Study of Songs Invented by Children Aged 5 to 7 Years. *British Journal of Music Education*, 9 (1), 19–48.

Davies, J. B., Kenny, P. and Barbenel, J. (1989). A Psychological Investigation of the Role of Mouthpiece Force in Trumpet Performance. *Psychology of Music*, 17, 48–62.

Fry, J. H. (1988). Patterns of Over-Use Seen in 658 Affected Instrumental Musicians. *International Journal of Music Education*, 11, 3–16.

Rainbow, B. (1967). *The Land Without Music*. London: Novello.

Rainbow, E. L. and Froehlich, H. C. (1987). *Research in Music Education*. New York: Schirmer.

Sloboda, J. A. (1991). Music Structure and Emotional Response: Some Empirical Findings. *Psychology of Music*, 19, 110–120.

Sloboda, J. A. and Howe, M. J. A. (1991). Biographical Precursors of Musical Excellence: An Interview Study. *Psychology of Music,* 19, 3–21.

Stake, R., Bresler, L. and Mabry, L. (1991). *Custom and Cherishing: The Arts in Elementary Schools.* Urbana, IL; Council for Research in Music Education/University of Illinois.

Wiersma, W. (1986). *Research Methods in Education.* (4th edn.) Newton, MA: Allyn and Bacon.

2

Historical Research

BERNARR RAINBOW

A sense of history, we have come to realize, forms a treasured feature of all productive cultures. For all but the most reckless of innovators historical awareness points the way ahead while affording safeguards against damaging excess; for the less mettlesome it extends inspiration and prompts courage to meet the challenge of the future. The truth of those claims is apparent in all fields of creative endeavour.

While perhaps more strikingly demonstrated within the fine arts the advantages conferred on the practitioner by knowledge of past practice and doctrine are also found in most other creative pursuits. The craft of teaching stands high among them and systematic examination of past aims, methods, and achievements within it offers a correspondingly fruitful and rewarding field for serious research.

It is usual in academic circles to refer to research of this calibre as designed 'to contribute to knowledge'. When conducted only at undergraduate level within an existing field of study, activity classed as research is customarily designed strictly for the student's own enlightenment. Though limited in scope, so long as it is honestly carried out and authentically reported, such modest research experience provides a desirable and useful preparation for later and more mature investigation. This in turn may at first be confined to circumscribed areas, the findings perhaps being published in the form of short articles or papers in appropriate journals.

More advanced and extended work at postgraduate levels will normally be conducted in more depth with greater rigour over a longer period of time and under the regular direction of an appointed supervisor. The contribution looked for now will be substantial, capable of influencing received opinion, and thence be 'deemed worthy of publication'.

Preliminary Considerations

Those who undertake historical research in the field of music education at higher levels must not allow the report they prepare of their eventual findings to relapse into imprecise narrative. This is best avoided at the outset by deliberately focusing attention on discoverable aims and procedures; by relating findings to current circumstances at home or abroad; by estimating revealed achievements and failures comparatively; and by meticulously recording all the sources drawn upon.

To fulfil all those requirements advanced students will need to undertake considerable preliminary reading. They must first become sufficiently aware of the educational scene as a whole to form a realistic estimate of the potential place and role of music teaching within it. They should make themselves familiar with the relevant findings of other researchers in the field so as to set their own results in perspective, both regionally and historically. Moreover, unless they become thoroughly conversant with the state of existing research in the chosen area their eventual personal discoveries may prove to be already familiar to scholars elsewhere.

Carefully conducted but narrowly-based research can founder through lack of background awareness. For instance, a student might attempt to investigate the influence of autocratic rule on educational policy as demonstrated in a particular regime. He or she would not find it too difficult to identify decrees uttered by Napoleon, for example, laying down ambitious programmes for the schools of France. But unless it was realized before closely examining and analysing those decrees that at the time in question there were too few competent teachers available in France to implement them their conclusions would be valueless.

Similarly a student might choose to examine the grandiose educational programmes introduced in Italy under Mussolini and then attempt to estimate their national impact. Before being able to reach a worthwhile conclusion he or she must have discovered that though elementary education in Italy had been made compulsory from 6 to 14 at the time in question, most of the nation's children stopped attending school at the age of eleven.

Selecting a Topic

The choice of a topic for research is not something to be undertaken hastily. If it is to prove fruitful the chosen subject should be one the investigator is prepared 'to live with' over the considerable period of time it requires to locate, assemble, and assess data and then submit the findings to rigorous testing before writing them up.

In practice the most fruitfully rewarding areas of research usually prove to have chosen themselves – because they arise from interests and enthusiasms already present and subsequently nourished in the minds of those undertaking them. In that respect it is hardly too fanciful to claim that historically-based research amounts to a form of inspired curiosity wedded to determined scrutiny of a type more usually associated with the great detectives of fiction.

Some mention of the sort of research question usefully addressed by historical methods may prove helpful here. An investigation relevant where the future development of music education is being considered – perhaps in a developing country – might involve comparison of past and present arguments advanced to support or oppose the admission of music lessons to the school curriculum.

At other levels the desirable content of the music curriculum, the choice of methods adopted to teach its component parts, and the wisdom or otherwise of available assessment procedures, all provide illuminating and potentially beneficial fields for historical investigation. Other topics inviting scrutiny which suggest themselves include the impact of social change on the choice of repertory, the effect on school music teaching of changing attitudes toward religious observance, or a comparison of the results of national preference for teaching *relative* as opposed to *fixed* sol-fa.

Less extensive topics relating to music teaching in schools and covering a smaller time-scale might concern varying attitudes toward children who cannot sing in tune, the influence of radio and television on school music lessons, or the impact on lesson content of the recent marked growth of instrumental teaching within the curriculum.

Topics relating to music teaching in schools perhaps provide the most inviting field for practising teachers to pursue; but equally rewarding areas of study present themselves within the territories of conservatory teaching and home-based musical study – as undertaken by adults as well as children.

Worthwhile findings produced after careful, well-authenticated research in these and many other areas can exert valuable influence where the modification and improvement of long standing procedures is being discussed. Indifferent practices often survive only because it occurs to no one to question them. Historical evaluation of procedures can aid improvement; it can equally justify the reinstatement of practices too hastily abandoned on questionable grounds.

At post-graduate level a programme of research must be capable of being studied to the depth required to justify the award of a higher degree. Here it is not just the student's intellectual ability that is in question. An equally decisive factor will be the likelihood of identifying and locating sufficient source material on which to base worthwhile enquiry.

Yet the student should not be discouraged too readily by an apparent shortage of suitable material. Diligent and patient investigators who acquire a feeling for tracking down source material will often find themselves developing something of the quality that Horace Walpole named 'serendipity' – *the faculty of making valuable discoveries by accident.* There is no shortage of anecdote on this subject among hardened researchers who enjoy telling how they found a critical report in a secondhand book-shop, or unexpectedly ran to earth an invaluable contemporary handwritten account in a basement lumber room.

Suffice to say that besides such inspired flukes an encouragingly large amount of material remains waiting to be extracted from surviving minute books, autobiographical memoirs, provincial and national newspapers and journals, library and college archives, government pronouncements, personal correspondence, and the like. Another invaluable source of historical information is to be found in outmoded textbooks. Long withdrawn from use in schools such books are not perhaps now so easily come by on secondhand bookstalls as was the case a generation or more ago; but they are still often to be found preserved in such specialist libraries as the Euing Collection at Glasgow University Library. An additional resource in this respect is the growing selection of such material at present being reproduced in facsimile in the series, *Classic Texts in Music Education,* published by Boethius Press and to be continued by Severinus Press, Newbury. (Certain of these items are endorsed CTME in the following booklist)

Compiling an Account

Earlier in this chapter regret was expressed that familiarity with the published results of research in music education remains regrettably thin among those it is intended to inform. It is difficult not to feel that much of the blame for this state of affairs rests with researchers themselves – for persistently framing their reports in such indigestible language.

It is not many years since Arnold Bentley first warned against the unnecessary use of 'jargon' in reporting research findings. Certain of the early research papers published in England at that time, dealing largely with the psychology of music and drawn up in many cases by non-musicians, seemed as uninviting to the practising music specialist as the arcane liturgy of some exclusive sect. The vogue since adopted in some quarters of affecting preposterous circumlocution when writing Ph.D theses and dissertations has done nothing to improve that situation.

It is greatly to be wished that this fashion be encouraged to lapse; and that what perhaps really amounts only to a candidate's anxiety to emphasize the intellectual respectability of his submission will cease to encourage the use of highfalutin language when compiling it. Research findings in the history of music education fortunately require neither elaborate terminology nor prolixity for their expression. They can as readily be stated in everyday terms immediately accessible to those whom they are meant to influence. General agreement among examiners and candidates to dispense with pretentious verbosity would help ensure that published findings reached teachers at large – instead of seeming to be the jealously guarded preserve of an inward-looking coterie.

The wisdom of making the findings of historical research inviting and interesting to the ordinary reader cannot be overstressed. One area where inexperienced research students may find themselves in doubt concerns the incorporation in a thesis of extended passages drawn from earlier treatises. If simply quoted verbatim these can prove highly indigestible. It is a good policy in such cases to limit direct quotation to passages where some individual feature – an original turn of phrase or an idiosyncratic term – justifies this treatment. For the rest, it is best to paraphrase and condense as far as possible. But when this is done the precise source of the material itself must always be cited.

History, declared Carlyle, is the essence of innumerable biographies. It is the essential humanity implied in that remark that is so often and so strikingly lacking from much current thesis writing. The turgid nature of most dissertations has led to a general assumption that before research findings merit publication in book form they must be entirely rewritten. Why, one asks, not write in readily readable form to begin with?

A Summary of Historical Research in Music Education

The different pace at which historically-based research in music education has developed in different countries is striking. It is possible to argue that the wide discrepancy found between the interest taken in research in neighbouring countries of Europe can to some extent be explained by differences of outlook and national temperament. However true that may be a complementary explanation also suggests itself.

The markedly different experience of formal music education enjoyed in each of those countries throughout the ages necessarily affects the occasion arising there for historical investigation. In German schools, for instance, systematic music teaching has flourished without interruption (despite some acknowledged lowering of standards during the 19th century) at least since Luther built upon medieval practice in the schools of the Reformation. Among her European neighbours no such long standing tradition is found. More usually the situation is one of long periods of neglect followed by sporadic though often energetic revival or reform.

That being so (and given the national temperament) in Germany there is no scarcity of historical discussion of music education. Elsewhere, however, it is more usually the introduction or re-introduction of music lessons in a country's schools that tends to spark off purposeful investigation of the scene in the past. Successive attempts to introduce music teaching in French, American, and English schools during the first half of the nineteenth century each produced isolated but important accounts of music teaching as it existed at home or abroad in former times. The situation in developing countries today suggests similar opportunities may arise there.

Against that background it would be invidious to attempt to draw up here a summary of each nation's contributions to historical research in what might readily be made to appear a league-table of achievement. To be compassable in a single chapter of the present book such a survey must inevitably be incomplete. It would consequently present individual countries with a misleading impression of their neighbours' activities while at the same time affording an inadequate picture of their own.

We have chosen instead to outline the situation that exists in the United Kingdom alone; and to do so by presenting a chronological list of representative articles and books published on the subject. In this way a realistic impression of the intermittent growth of research in this field in a single country – a pattern not unlikely to be found also elsewhere – can be recorded. The titles of some standard works published in other countries have then been added at the conclusion.

Starting in the 1840s with a handful of examples, early investigations in Britain accompanied and were stimulated by individual efforts to re-introduce music teaching in schools. Many of these investigations were conducted by the innovators themselves for their own guidance. Later in the century research specifically dealing with music education is rare; but incidental references to music teaching can be found tucked away in such classic treatises on the general educational scene as A.T. Drane's *Christian Schools and Scholars* (1867), A.F. Leach's *History of Winchester College* (1899) and *Educational Charters and Documents* (1911).

Attention returned to the subject when plans for post-war development led to the formal review of many aspects of national life during World War II. Educational reform and the need to make detailed plans for its implementation occupied an important place in that debate. The general mood of earnestness and need for action – in music education as elsewhere – stimulated some modest research into past practice and a second wave of publications dealing specifically with the history of music teaching in schools now began.

The first investigations concerned the medieval and renaissance periods – and perhaps strike an observer today as musicological exercises in escapism rather than attempts to reveal foundations on which to rebuild a modern scheme of music education. But the mood changed and strengthened as the centenary of the founding of the *Musical Times* in 1944 inspired the publication of Percy Scholes' remarkable two-volume digest of the musical progress of the nation.

The Mirror of Music, as his study was called, gave pride of place in its pages to the singing-class movement of the 1840s – a movement whose activities the *Musical Times* itself had first been designed to record. One of Scholes' subsequent chapters traced the history and growth of 'Music in the Nation's Schools'.

Following the impetus provided by Percy Scholes' conspectus a few further articles on the subject began to appear. The first considerable texts then followed in the

1960s heralding a literature that has since shown signs of growing more substantial. It is from examination of all these publications – not forgetting their often extensive Bibliographies – and from such former journals as the *Tonic Sol-fa Reporter,* the *Musical Herald,* the *School Music Review, Music in Education,* and the *Music Teacher,* that serious students will be able to equip themselves with the necessary background material needed to pursue research of the type and quality this chapter is designed to encourage.

Some Conclusions

Research in music education may take the form of experimental or quantitative analysis, philosophical enquiry or historical investigation. Most participants today are attracted to work within the scientifically-based areas. That preponderance, so understandably in tune with the spirit of a technological age, has perhaps been allowed to suggest too readily that research in music education is only justified when it provides scientific answers to current problems.

The present chapter was invited with a suggestion from the editor that it should describe the kinds of question which historical methods are most able to address. That condition has been accepted and some answers supplied. Yet it is desirable here to emphasize that it is also a function of historical research – and one at least equally important in the opinion of many observers – to compile and furnish an accurate record of past events intended purely for present enlightenment.

In this instance that course involves describing how and why former procedures were evolved that contributed toward laying the foundation of the modern music curriculum. It also involves describing the aims, achievements and failures of pioneer music teachers – all of them empirical rather than theoretical endeavours and concerned with real schools replete with real children. The beneficial influence on present-day teachers of an awareness of their predecessors' efforts to achieve what we have all in turn inherited should not be underestimated. Indeed, many students and teachers whose temperament leaves them untouched by the results of statistical research find themselves edified and inspired by discovering the emergent background of their craft. If for no other reason than this, historical and scientific research are wisely to be regarded as complementary.

But there must be a proviso. Scientific research carries its own implicit mathematical infallibility. Historical research deserves equal esteem only so far as its findings prove equally reliable. For that to happen there can be no juggling of material to fit predetermined conclusions; no omission of inconvenient or uncomfortable data. Truth, not just meeting the routine academic requirements for the award of a degree, must be the investigator's goal.

Ultimate findings satisfying those conditions deserve to be carefully written up with due sense of pride. History, after all, has long and rightly been regarded as a form of literature.

A List of British Publications

Part One 1842–1900

Hickson, W. E. Music, and the Committee of Council on Education. *Westminster Review*, XXXVII, no. 1, pp. 11ff, Jan 1842.

Mainzer, J. *Music and Education*. Edinburgh: A. & C. Black. London: Longman, Brown and Green, 1848, R/1984 (CTME).

Curwen, J. Introduction, *Singing for Schools & Congregations: A Grammar of Vocal Music.* London: Curwen, 1848 R/1985 (CTME).

Curwen, J. History and Statistics in *The Teacher's Manual.* London, 1875 R/19986 (CTME).

Macfarren, C. A. *Addresses and Lectures.* London: Curwen, 1888.

Marr, R. *Music for the People.* Edinburgh: Menzies, 1889.

Part Two 1900–1992

Harris, D. G. T. Musical Education in Tudor Times. *PRMA,* 27 April, 1939.

Thompson, A. H. *Song Schools in the Middle Ages.* London, 1942.

Scholes, P. A. *The Mirror of Music,* 2 vols. London: Novello, 1947.

Sternfield, F. W. Music in the Schools of the Reformation. *Musica Disciplina,* II, Rome, 1948.

Rainbow, B. An Excellency in Musick. *The Journal of Education,* vol. 89, no. 1056 July 1957.

Dobbs, J. P. B. *Three Pioneers of Sight-Singing in the 19th century.* Newcastle: Institute of Education, 1964.

Rainbow, B. The Historical and Philosophical Background of School Music Teaching, in *Handbook for Music Teachers.* London: Novello, 1964, R/1968.

Le Huray, P. The Teaching of Music in 16th-century England. *Music in Education,* Mar/April, 1966.

Rainbow, B. *The Land without Music: musical education in England 1800–1860 & its continental antecedents.* London: Novello, 1967 R/1991.

Simpson, K. *Some Great Music Educators.* London: Novello, 1976.

Rainbow, B. *English Psalmody Prefaces: popular methods of instruction, 1562 1835.* Kilkenny: Boethius, 1982, (CTME).

Cant, S. Women Composers and the Music Curriculum. *British Journal of Music Education,* 7 (1), 5–14, March 1990.

Southcott, J. A Music Education Pioneer – Dr Satis Naronna Barton Coleman, *British Journal of Music Education,* 7 (2), 123–132, July 1990.

Rainbow, B. *Music in Educational Thought & Practice.* Aberystwyth: Boethius, 1991.

Rainbow, B. *Music and the English Public School.* Aberystwyth: Boethius, 1991 (CTME).

Some Standard Works Published Elsewhere

United States of America

Birge, E. B. *A History of Public School Music in the United States.* Philadelphia: Oliver Ditson, 1937.

Britton, A. P. Music Education: an American Speciality, in *One Hundred Years of Music in America,* ed. P.H. Lang, NY, 1961.

Bernarr Rainbow

Tellstrom, A. T. *Music in American Education, Past and Present.* New York: Holt, Rinehart and Winston, 1971.

Keene, J. A. *A History of Music Education in the United States.* UP of New England, 1982.

Australia and New Zealand

Bartle, G. *Music in Australian Schools.* Melbourne, 1968.

Tait, M. J. *Music Education in New Zealand.* Hamilton, 1970.

Bridges, D. Some Historical Backgrounds to Australian Music Education. *Australian Journal of Music Education,* 1974.

Canada

Beckwith, J. Music Education, in *Encyclopedia Canadiana,* vii, Toronto, 1957.

Walter, A. The Growth of Music Education, in *Aspects of Music in Canada* Toronto, 1969.

France

Clarval, J. A. *L'ancienne maîtrise de Notre-Dame de Chartres du Ve Siècle à la révolution,* Paris, 1899.

Chevais, M. L'enseignement musical à l'école, in *Encyclopedie de la Musique,* ed. Lavignac et Laurencie, Paris, 1925.

Germany

Kretzschmar, H. *Musikalische Zeitfragen.* Leipzig: Peters, 1903.

Schunemann, G. *Geschichte des Schulgesang unterrichts.* Berlin, 1913.

Braun, G. *Die Schulmusikerziehung in Preussen von den Falkschen Bestimmungen bis zur Kestenberg-Reform.* Kassel and Basle, 1957.

Abel-Struth, S. Materialien zur Entwicklung der Musikpädagogik als Wissenschaft. In S. Abel-Struth (ed.) *Musikpädagogik, Forschung und Lehre, Vol. 1.* Mainz, 1970.

Abel-Struth, S. Aktualitat und Geschichtsbewußtsein in der Musikpädagogik. In S. Abel-Struth (ed.) *Musikpädagogik, Forschung und Lehre, Vol. 9.* Mainz, 1973.

Hopf, H., Heise, W. and Helms, S. *Lexikon der Musikpädagogik.* Regensburg: Gustav Bosse Venlag, 1984.

Switzerland

Cherbuliez, A. E. *Geschichte der Musikpädagogik in der Schweiz,* 1944.

(See also the article Education in Music in the *New Grove Dictionary of Music and Musicians,* S. Sadie (ed), vol. 6. London, 1980).

3

Comparative Research

LAURENCE LEPHERD

Whenever music educators observe any aspect of music education in one situation and try to determine if it can be applied in their own, they are comparing. In any comparison there is a need to identify what is being compared, and to select or develop the most appropriate comparative methods. This kind of research addresses the questions of how ideas, found in one situation, can be taken and successfully applied in another, and how comparisons can be made so that the conclusions reached are both reliable and valid.

There are many ways in which comparisons can be approached. There are, for example, thematic comparisons. One theme may consist of the study of group instrumental teaching strategies in different elementary schools within a locality or between localities. Another may involve assessment procedures in music conservatories. In each case the music educator has to find the relevant literature, observe the action, make comparisons and record conclusions in a systematic manner. Another kind of comparison may involve ethnographic studies dealing with different cultural groups requiring specific methods which enable rigorous human observational techniques to be used. A further description of these methods may be found in Lepherd (1998a). A more detailed analysis of the development of comparative and international music education in the last forty years can be found in Kemp and Lepherd (1992).

Another basis for comparison relates to national systems of music education. Reference is often made to music education in the United States, Japan or Hungary, and generalizations stated about what takes place in these countries. Whilst it may be very stimulating to observe provisions for music education in such nation-states, there is danger in engaging in indiscriminate 'cross-cultural borrowing', that is, taking ideas from one context and trying to place them in a completely different context without really considering the factors which influence the provision of music education in the respective systems. The importance of culture and cultural differences has been the subject of considerable discussion by comparative educationists. Significant reference to the work of Jullien, Hans, and Mallinson, pioneers in the field, is made in Jones (1971). King (1968), Noah and Eckstein (1969), Holmes (1981) and Epstein (1988) are among many others who have also addressed the issue.

Nation-state comparison has been an element in the comparative methodology debate since the beginning of modern comparative studies in the nineteenth century. While there has been criticism of this form of comparison over the last two decades, such a basis still has a relatively recent recognition (Holmes, 1981; Postlethwaite, 1988). One of the greatest difficulties in nation-state comparison is the development of a conceptual framework which enables the standardization of an analysis of national systems, and which uses a method which facilitates their systematic comparison. The framework should assist in the making of informed judgements based on an interpretation of data collected and the consideration of factors relevant to the different contexts.

A Model for Analysis and Comparison

One conceptual framework which can be used for the analysis and comparison of music education in national systems is adapted from the work of Holmes (1981) and Bereday (1966 and 1967). Holmes has suggested six categories in such a model.

The first aspect of education which it is logical to address is that of *aims* because it is recognized that education should have purpose. Aims are usually expressed at different levels of education starting with such policy documents as a national constitution, and continuing in more specific terms through provincial legislation, local curricula, influential music educators and professional associations. Aims can be found in three sub-classifications. *Child centred* aims are those in which the child is the focus of education. *Society centred* aims are those in which education is seen as the means through which society is developed. *Subject centred* aims relate to the way in which the continued development of the subject is considered to be of paramount importance. In reality, aims of education can rarely be categorized absolutely in these terms. In music education all three aims can be expressed in various documents and the comparative interest is in the degree of emphasis placed on each.

The second category presented by Holmes is *administration*. He suggests that after aims are expressed and promoted nationally they need to be implemented. Governments develop administrative systems which assist in this implementation. Administrative systems usually encompass three levels – national, provincial and local. Description of a system involves identifying the relationship between these levels, particularly observing the various responsibilities associated with each.

In order to implement any education there is a need for *finance*. Comparative interest is in the way in which finance is provided, who provides it, and how it is expended. This generally includes government provision at the system level and can include commercial, philanthropic and parental provision. An important issue in financial considerations is accountability and related to this is system evaluation.

The next level of interest is associated with the *structure and organization* of education. This involves an analysis of the educational continuum from early childhood through to tertiary institutions and adult education. Of particular interest is the way in which provision is made for music at each level, how transition from one level to another is facilitated, and how progression is assessed.

The fifth category concerns *curricula*. Once the aims have been determined, the provision made for administration, sources of finance determined and the structure established, the curricula for all levels (from pre-school to higher and adult education) need to be developed. Curriculum design includes the formation of specific objectives for music education, and the content and learning strategies for each level of instruction. Holmes has identified three theories into which curricula generally fall. These are *essentialism* – the question of what subjects are essential for general education, *encyclopedism* – the assertion that all knowledge should be found in a curriculum, and *pragmatism* – the consideration of what is important to overcome the problem of living. This analysis can be applied to music curricula. The presence of music for all children aged 6–12 years, for example, suggests essentialism. The nature of curriculum content would determine if the curriculum was encyclopedic – if all aspects of music were in the curriculum, or pragmatic – if there was an emphasis on the teaching of social skills, or developing specific society aims. Of further interest is curriculum development – how it is carried out and who is involved.

The final category suggested by Holmes is that of *teacher education*. Curricula need implementation. How teachers are trained to implement both before and during employment is of comparative interest. Before employment the issues of length, type and balance of courses, and methods of assessment are important. During employment, types of teacher and teacher status, promotion and professional development opportunities are important considerations. Holmes has developed this model for analysis with the view to standardizing the method of presentation of national systems. Standardization facilitates comparison because the variables can be identified.

George Bereday, however, some years previously, developed a comparative method which can be used in conjunction with Holmes' model and with a further extension, enables even more rigorous comparison. Bereday suggests that national systems can be compared in four stages. It is important to describe and interpret a system first. Initially, Bereday suggested that these two processes should be sequential but in practice he found that it was more appropriate for them to be undertaken simultaneously. Description and interpretation can be carried out using the Holmes' model. Once this process has been completed the third stage of juxtaposition and preliminary comparison can be carried out. In this process data can be placed side-by-side to determine comparability. This will also involve rejecting data which, for a variety of reasons including 'not applicable', can be determined. The fourth stage involves comparison proper, that is, after the comparable data have been determined detailed comparison can take place.

One of Bereday's principles is that the data to be described is interpreted in the light of the variety of factors which influence the education process which can include sociological, economic, historical and geographical considerations. It can be more appropriate to review the factors before examining the provisions for music education.

In music education there is also a real need to examine the musical context of the society. This includes the nature of the music – a nation's traditional music as well as other forms, and also the current national climate for music – the extent to which national or local organizations of a variety of kinds influence directly the provisions for music education. Within this framework it is possible to establish a link between the educational context, the musical context and the direct provisions. Music education does not exist in a vacuum. A nation's system is the way it is because of the factors which have influenced its development. Often the factors differ from one country to another and it is important to recognize this in the description and interpretation, and, above all, the comparison.

One method which can be used in collecting data for a description of national systems is ethnographic. Wiersma (1986) defines ethnographic research as 'the process of providing scientific descriptions of educational systems, processes, and phenomena within specific contexts' (p.233). The above model provides a framework for a scientific, that is, accurate and testable description of educational systems within specific contexts.

The Research Process

The Literature Search

The first step in the collection of data is to obtain an overview of the context. This involves a literature search of relevant data. The breadth and currency of sources is extremely important. These include:

> Official government publications
> Encyclopedias, monographs and journals
> Media publications – newspaper articles, videos
> Discussions with music educators at all levels of education

It is important to obtain access to primary sources. It is valuable to obtain publications in the original language and have them translated independently where possible. It is vital to obtain a range of views – from government publications to journal, and media articles. The reason for this is that often there is a gap between the official government policy and the way in which it is implemented or perceived by educators.

Once the overview has been obtained a literature search of similar documents in music education is necessary. (In reality this often overlaps because music education articles can also be found in the same vicinity as the general education articles.) Again, the same principles apply with an emphasis on the primary sources moderated by informed comment available through journals and other sources.

The Field Study

Once the initial literature search has been completed and the researcher has developed an awareness of the parameters of music education provision, arrangements need to be made for the carrying out of the field work. This usually involves the obtaining of official permission to visit institutions. The literature search should have revealed information for the six categories used in analysis and provide an idea of the kind of institutions to be visited. Where possible it is important to visit a range of institutions. The difficulty with 'Official Permission' is that officials will often arrange for visits to the 'show' institutions. This is understandable. However, music education is not only about the way some colleagues have developed good programmes, but about the identification, analysis and solution of problems. Any field work should be undertaken from the perspective of considering the broad spectrum of the realities of music education.

During the field study it is useful to employ two different techniques of observation. It is important to know what to look for so that a series of structured questions and observations can be developed. The observations can be made of classes and students, and questions asked of teachers and other colleagues. However, too much structuring can result in an inflexible approach to the collection of data. It is often useful to probe with broad questions first to allow for 'hidden' agenda to emerge. It is vital to recognize these when they do appear so that a more specific follow-up can be made. Each visit should be carefully documented and consistently reviewed against the data collected in the literature search to ensure that the field work is rigorous and that new material which emerges in the field work can be appropriately placed in the model and further investigated if necessary.

A useful device in questioning is the picking out of key concepts, some of which may be controversial. The highlighting of a controversial topic in a number of different situations can be very enlightening, particularly when opposing views are promulgated.

The Report

When the literature search and the field work are completed it is possible to commence the report writing. An advantage of the model outlined is that it enables data to be sifted from a variety of places and classified appropriately. When on field work it is important to develop relations with a variety of colleagues which will enable follow up questions to be asked. These colleagues may also assist in the verification and interpretation of data presented in the report.

The Problems

There are always problems in comparative analyses. The greatest of these is ensuring that the data collected are comparable. Any terms used must be defined because the same terms can have different meanings in different countries. A similar problem exists in trying to handle quantitative data. Conducting surveys based on the same questions can have little value if the questions asked are understood differently in different contexts.

Overcoming cultural bias is another difficulty. Critical analysis of national systems should lead to informed judgements. But, by what standard should the critical analysis be made? It is not always appropriate in comparative research to make value judgements based on the researcher's own values, or assumptions. It is preferable that the comparative analyst documents the criticisms of colleagues within the national systems being described. In this way the researcher becomes the recorder of provisions and criticism, facilitating judgements to be made by others.

Another difficulty in using the model outlined above is in relation to financial provisions. The method of documenting the collection and expending of funds for music education varies considerably within countries as well as between countries. There is a need to try to develop a model for financial analysis which overcomes these problems.

A further problem in ethnographic research is in sampling and generalizing. In national systems there are often sub-systems, particularly when a nation consists of a number of autonomous states or provinces each with a variety of different provisions. The problem of generalizing across a nation involves an analysis of the variety of provisions and a statement of the commonalities and differences. The differences are evident right across the six categories of the model for analysis. For example, aims: there may be a national statement of the aims of education but not of music education. At national levels statements are usually very generalized. However, in music education, whilst governments may not articulate the aims of music education a consensus of the aims expressed in autonomous regions may indicate a prevailing commonality. A national professional association may also provide substantiation of this. An important consideration, however, is that description should not be reduced to a measure satisfactory to the researcher but should be an indication of what exists. If this means stating that a national system of, say, ten autonomous regions has an expression of aims which involve commonality in seven and distinct differences in the other three, then it is important to describe the situation in this way.

One final problem: a major danger in the use of a systematic model for analysis is that in an endeavour to rigorously describe the system, ensure accuracy and comparability, and fit everything in its analytical pigeonhole, it is possible to miss seeing important issues which cut across all categories. These issues must be addressed and described in each of the categories as is relevant.

An Example of Analysis and Preliminary Comparison

To demonstrate some of the above principles a brief analysis and preliminary comparison will be made of three countries: the People's Republic of China; Australia; and the Soviet Union. Data relating to each country was collected before August 1991. While the context may have changed in each country, particularly with the demise of the Soviet Union and the establishment of the Commonwealth of Independent States, the principles of comparison are still relevant. The context for music education, and each country's current status of music before 1991 will be described. Reference will then be made to the first of Holmes' categories, the aims of music education, and preliminary comparative conclusions will be drawn (the third stage of Bereday's comparative method). A complete comparative study would involve a similar analysis of the other five categories, namely, administration, finance, structure and organization, curricula and teacher education.

The Context for Music Education

China: China has over 1,000 million people. These are distributed over 56 ethnic groups which means that Chinese society is multi-cultural. One group, the Han, comprise 94% of the population. Contemporary society is characterized by what is known as the four modernizations for economic development to the year 2000. In order to enable China to take its place alongside other industrialized countries, emphasis is being placed on achieving rapid growth in science and technology, industry, agriculture and national defence. Education is regarded as one of the most important ways of assisting in the achievement of these modernizations.

Culturally, China has centuries of history and tradition which influence a considerable amount of the people's activity and values. There is a belief in the need for centralist government and conformity. It is contended that the aim to further develop a communist and socialist ethos can best be achieved through central control and legislation. Provincial (regional) governments reflect the policies developed centrally.

Australia: Australia is a relatively small country in population consisting of only 16 million people. It is multi-cultural because it consists of the earliest inhabitants (the Aborigines), people of British ancestry who emigrated after European settlement in the late 18th century, Europeans who emigrated from their war-torn countries after 1945, and Asians who have arrived in small numbers since first settlement but in larger numbers since the end of the Vietnam war. The relative shortness of European settlement and the small population has resulted in a short tradition and constant change to the extent that reference is made more to Australian cultures rather than Australian culture.

Federal and state (provincial) governments are responsible for the development and implementation of policies but have defined boundaries. State rights are jealously guarded. Primary and secondary education are the responsibilities of the state governments.

Soviet Union: Before August 1991 the Soviet Union consisted of 15 autonomous Republics linked by a common communist and socialist ethos. The total population was 282.4 million and it was multi-national because the Republics were largely based around nationalities. The most populous Republic was the Russian Soviet Federated Socialist Republic which comprises 50% of the total population of the Union. The Republics of the Union have long traditions but the Union itself only existed this century. Political events during the period of communist domination have been frequently regarded as having had an adverse effect on the development of music. Policies were developed centrally and enforced in the Republics.

Two well publicized traits of recent Soviet society were *glasnost* – openness, and *perestroika* – restructuring. These terms were generally applied to all facets of Soviet life and included music education. The principle was that people were encouraged to be open in their constructive criticism of Soviet society so that progress could be made in restructuring, an implied admission that the implementation of communist principles as had been known was not successful.

Music

China: Chinese music is rich in tradition. It has centuries of development in both vocal and instrumental music. Vocally, there are literally thousands of folk songs. Conservatories are currently engaged in the huge task of collecting, classifying and transcribing folk music from the various regions. Folk instruments reflect the centuries of trade with other countries so that many of the traditional instruments owe their basic origins to the West but have undergone uniquely Chinese changes.

Whilst there are the folk songs and traditional instrumental musics of China, the centuries-old Chinese opera demonstrates the concept of the integration of the arts. Chinese opera is more well-known through its regional variations, the most well-known being Peking (or Beijing) opera. In this art form instruments, voice and dance combine in a unique ensemble which reflects traditional Chinese civilisation.

Given the difficult economic circumstances of China, there are few entrepreneurial organizations whose task it is to promote musical culture. There are, however, many musical companies who directly market their own performances. They are often assisted by central and regional governments.

Despite the traditional music, the move towards modernization has had an important influence on current musical development. The opening up of society to western ideas has had a dramatic affect on music through the importing of western 'pop' music. This has resulted in the development of what is known as 'Sino-pop' music – the local variation. This in turn is influencing music in China's schools. One of the more conscious problems in China's musical development is that the push for modernization has also meant a desire to move towards more European music in schools. The prevalence of violins, flutes and electronic keyboards has been promoted to the detriment of traditional instruments. The decline of widespread interest in traditional music is also reflected, for example, in the observation that attendance at performances of Chinese opera consists mostly of older people and tourists.

Australia: Australia's short European history has resulted in a short tradition in music. Early musical development was associated with the arrival of European, essentially British, immigrants. These were largely of three kinds: the convicts and then poorer settlers who brought with them the folk songs of their own regions, the service personnel who constantly used military music, and the more affluent who brought their church choral, and piano music backgrounds with them. The consequence of this was a colourful folk heritage which became adapted to the sometimes harsh realities of Australian life, and an artistic development centred around British life with music education modelled on current British practices. Music retained a separate existence, it was rarely integrated with other arts.

Existing alongside this development was the bare survival of aboriginal music. This was closely related to dance and the combination was closely related to functional aspects of tribal life. Originally, and for many decades, seen as primitive, aboriginal culture is now receiving greater recognition, and genuine attempts are being made to maintain it in its original form as well as to recognize the changes taking place because of the urbanization of many aboriginals, and the influences of contemporary society.

Currently, considerable emphasis is given to entre-preneurial activities. Semi-government agencies are re-sponsible for musical promotion ranging from traditional, multi-cultural music, to opera, ballet and instrumental music of various styles. There is considerable British and American influence evident in the wider musical scene through promotion in the popular media.

Soviet Union: The extensive history associated with the various Republics resulted in a long cultural tradition. The twentieth century communist dominance, however, demonstrated a controlled growth in the quantity and quality of musical culture. Tight guidelines on what con-stituted acceptable musical expression resulted in a nar-row concept of music. A consequence of the pursuit of excellence was the development of a remarkable and inter-nationally renowned musical standard in the European classical genre. Individual Republics pursued excellence in their traditional music. However, the insular nature of communist dominance generally resulted in narrow expression. The repression of religion resulted in little religious music. Lack of international contact resulted in little awareness of the traditional music of other countries.

The prevalence of *glasnost* led to the desire for reform but the existence of the increasingly unpopular *perestroika* caused frustration. The desire for reform in music education could not be matched by action because of economic constraints and entrenched conservative attitudes.

There were two main influences on music education coming from outside the education system. The first was found in *palaces of culture*, and the second, the *Union of Composers*. Palaces were established by organizations of workers to assist in the cultural (and musical) development of children and adults. The decreasing influence of communism resulted in the lessening of the influence of these organizations.

The Union of Composers retained a strong influence on the development of classical music, particularly in the school and conservatory system. But this organization also, in a society being increasingly influenced by modern and popular music, was being criticized for its lack of flexibility.

Aims

The following excerpts are taken from official sources, i.e. government documents or officially recognized individuals, and refer to the general aims of education and music education.

China: After the social upheaval of the Cultural Revolution in the 1970s and in the early 1980s, the Education Ministry took steps to strengthen the ideological work of schools. One expressed aim was to 'build up students' confidence in socialism and foster in them the communist spirit and morality' (China Handbook Editorial Committee, 1983). Government policy regarded music education as one of the most important means of achieving aesthetic development. Music education honourably develops a student's heart, mind and resourcefulness. It is indispensable for this. It will improve the level of science and culture of the nation and will serve in the accomplishment of the Four Modernisations. (Ministry of Education, 1985)

A respected Chinese music educator wrote:

Music education is a component part in the development of a student in an all-round way – morally, intellectually and physically. Music education must assist in bringing up a new generation in the socialist construction of a spiritual civilisation. (Wang Ke, 1983)

Australia: Aims expressed in a State (provincial) music education curriculum are:

The central aim of education which, with home and community groups, the school pursues, is to guide individual development in the context of society through recognisable stages of development towards perceptive understanding, mature judgement, responsible self-direction and moral autonomy. (Department of Education NSW, 1983)

The aims expressed in a curriculum resource book in the State of Victoria are:

To nurture in children an enjoyment and understanding of music which will enrich the quality of their lives.
    To help children realise their potential by providing opportunities for creativity and expression of feelings and ideas through music. (Education Department of Victoria, 1981)

Soviet Union: Article 25 of the USSR Constitution states that the country should have:

a uniform system of public education, which shall be constantly improved, that provides general education and vocational training for citizens, serves communist education and the intellectual and physical development of youth, and trains them for working life and social activity. (Cited in Onuchkine, 1985)

The respected musician and music educator, Dimitri Kabalevsky wrote:

In any serious matter, one must begin with the very deepest foundations of our life, and, in this instance, with an understanding of the role played by esthetic upbringing, and musical upbringing in particular, in the development of society. In so doing, it should be borne in mind that an esthetic evaluation always amounts to an ethical evaluation, and assists in the shaping of humanistic qualities in the individual. Every society therefore determines the scale and direction of esthetic upbringing according to its own image and likeness. (Kabalevsky, 1988)

An example of the application of *glasnost* can be found in the following:

At the moment we are having to cope with the situation in which people are not the real goal of education but have been reduced to some sort of means or material, an inert body to be acted upon. There is an urgent and fundamental need to overcome the absence of adequate conditions for the development and self-realisation of the creative personality. (Mironova, 1989)

A Preliminary Comparison – Aims

The fundamental issue in considering the aims of education and music education in any national system is recognizing the tension which exists between achieving

51

individual development, the development of society and an increase in the body of knowledge. Rarely are the statements of any aims going to be pigeon-holed only into any one of the categories. The real interest is the relative emphasis placed on each.

After reading the above expressions, there is little doubt that in China the emphasis in the aims of music education are society centred. Within the context described earlier covering immense population, communist philosophy and centralist controlled development, such emphasis is not unexpected. If the analysis was to go further, it would be seen that the administration, financial control, structure, curricula and teacher education provisions reflect this emphasis. For example, curriculum content, particularly at primary school level, is uniform throughout the nation. Each primary school uses the same set of books which are applied to each grade throughout the whole of the country. Secondary music education has similar principles, the exception being that the books used are developed at provincial level rather than at national level. Teaching strategies are similarly uniform and reflect the aims. Classroom practices are very teacher-oriented, designed to develop the class as a whole rather than the individuals within it, at least as officially practised. In reality, there is a sub-conscious eulogising of individuals, the success of the individual teacher often being measured by the high standard of some individuals in the class.

The evident emphasis in the aims of Australian music education is on individual development. This reinforces a principle that it is the individual's right to have the best opportunity to develop to the limit of capability. The tension becomes evident when it is also advocated that individuals should recognize the role they are expected to play in society. Again, within context, considerable provincial administrative, financial and curricular autonomy in at least primary and secondary school education is commensurate with aims.

In the Soviet Union, the dramatically changing societal and political context is inexorably affecting music education. The official aims stated in the Constitution and endorsed by Kabalevsky, equally official because of his high status, show the dichotomy. The official statements espouse communism. Kabalevsky espoused the need for the continued development of socialism but saw it as being through the development of individuals. He recognized the importance of individual expression which contributed to the development of the art and to society.

In reality, in the changing context and the advent of *glasnost*, the officially expressed aims are being held less and less with high regard. Mironova (1989) illustrates some current concerns with the practice of 'mass production'. The tension evident here is that whilst conservatively, the aims are concerned with the development of a good socialist society, and whilst some individuals want to achieve the development of more individualism, the administrative, economic, organizational structures, curriculum content and strategies, and teacher education provisions are not facilitating this. This point illustrates another problem in analysis and highlights the necessity for a broad spectrum of input into the collection of data. The problem concerns the differences which can exist between official policy and actual practice.

Implications for Comparative Studies

The intention of the above is to demonstrate that comparative music education studies must be carried out with considerable regard for broader societal and educational contexts. To take an aim, or a financial provision, or a curriculum strategy, out of its context and try to place it in another can lead to incompatibility and is similar to organ rejection in medical transplants. A systematic study of context and provisions, and use of a comparative method which identifies variables can lead to a more informed prediction of success in the implementation of an idea in a different context.

It is emphasized that what has been described is but one approach to comparative music education study. One of the criticisms of nation-state comparison is that it is highly complex. There are so many internal and external variables related to music education that it becomes extremely difficult to identify and collect the most relevant data, to analyse and interpret it, and then make useful comparisons which lead to progress.

Nevertheless, such a study is important because it provides an initial overview of relevant data within defined parameters which can be useful in the more detailed study of single variables or themes. It assists in identifying issues which are common to different countries. By analysing these issues systematically within their respective context and observing the way in which solutions are attempted, insight can be gained into strategies for problem solution.

Systematic comparative study in music education is in its infancy. There has been a welcome proliferation of international studies since the early 1950s but few of these have been directly comparative. Building on the work and debate of comparative educationists should provide a firmer basis for more beneficial studies in comparative music education.

References

Bereday, G. Z. F. (1966). *Comparative Method in Education*. New York: Holt, Rinehart and Winston.

Bereday, G. Z. F. (1967). Reflections in Comparative Methodology in Education 1964–1966. *Comparative Education Review*, 3, 1, 169–187.

China Handbook Editorial Committee (1983). *Education and Science – China Handbook Series*. Beijing: Foreign Languages Press.

Department of Education New South Wales (1983). *Aims of Primary Education in New South Wales*. Sydney: Department of Education, New South Wales.

Epstein, E. H. (1988). The Problematic Meaning of 'Comparison' in Comparative Education. In J. Schriewer and B. Holmes (eds.), *Theories and Methods in Comparative Education*. Frankfurt am Main: Peter Lang.

Education Department of Victoria (1981). *A Guide to Music in the Primary School*. Education Department of Victoria, Publications and Information Branch.

Holmes, B. (1981). *Comparative Education: Some Considerations of Method*. London: George Allen & Unwin.

Jones, P. E. (1971). *Comparative Education: Purpose and Method*. Brisbane: University of Queensland Press.

Kabalevsky D. (1988). On Restructuring with Optimism but Without Embellishment. *Soviet Education*, XXX 1, 9.

Kemp, A. and Lepherd, L. (1992). Research Methods in International and Comparative Music Education. In Richard Colwell (ed.), *Handbook for Research in Music Teaching and Learning*. New York: Schirmer.

Lepherd, L. (1988a). The Challenge of Viewing World Music Education. *International Music Education*, ISME Yearbook Volume XV, pp. 131–135.

Lepherd, L. (1988b). *Music Education in International Perspective: The People's Republic of China*. Darling Heights: Music International.

Ministry of Education (1985). *A Collection of Teaching Programmes for Music Education in Primary and Secondary Schools issued from 1949–1985*. Beijing: Ministry of Education.

Mironova, N. (1989). Musical Education: Methods and Problems of Restructuring. In V. P. Fomin et al (eds.), *Musical Education – Individual Personality – Culture*. The P. I. Tchaikovsky State Conservatory of Music, Moscow, pp. 3–25. (Translated by R Woodhouse, University of Queensland, Australia.)

Noah, H. J. and Eckstein, M. A. (1969). *Toward a Science of Comparative Education*. London: Macmillan.

Postlethwaite, T. N. (ed.) (1988). *The Encyclopedia of Comparative Education and National Systems of Education*. Oxford: Pergamon.

Onuchkine, V. G. (1985). The Problems and Forms of Interaction between School and Out-of-School Education in the USSR. *Report Studies*. Paris: UNESCO.

Wang Ke (1983). *Music Teaching in the Middle School*. Beijing: People's Music Press.

Wiersma, W. (1986). *Research Methods in Education: An Introduction*. Massachusetts: Allyn and Bacon.

4

Experimental Research

HAROLD E. FISKE

Music education employs experimental research procedures in order to test hypotheses about the effectiveness of music teaching materials and teaching strategies. Experimental research is the practical outcome of inductive reasoning; it is founded on the premise that predictions of (musical) behaviour may be made by systematically observing and comparing the (musical) behaviour of a representative few. The more representative the observations, the more likely that the predictions made from these observations will be fulfilled.

Since the publication of Hermann von Helmholtz's book *On the Sensations of Tones* (1863) we have seen considerable growth in the number of experimental researchers. There has also been a concomitant growth in research skill, technique, and sophistication, accompanied by a steady increase in attention from the larger music education research community.

This surge of interest has, however, led to complaints from non-researchers about the relevance of certain research areas to the day-to-day concerns of music teachers; there is some concern that the 'real' problems of teaching music are not considered by researchers, and that the results of studies confined to a few classrooms or schools may not generalize to other teaching situations. However, these complaints often reflect a critic's misunderstanding about the research process itself. I am not going to pursue these issues here (but see Heller & Campbell, 1985). Instead, I am going to offer an alternative strategy: teachers should become their *own* researchers. By serving as their own researchers teachers can select research problems germane to their current teaching activities and interests. Also, teachers who conduct research usually use their own students as subjects; they know, therefore, whose musical abilities the results are about.

Research Practice Versus Teaching Practice

There are two ways in which researchers operate differently from teachers. First, researchers tend to be more systematic than teachers. Although teachers also ask questions, formulate hypotheses, make observations, and compare results, the procedures tend to be less formal than those accepted by researchers. Researchers are trained to analyse questions in ways that enable them to organize observation conditions such that manipulation of variables offers the greatest potential for providing reliable and valid information.

Second, music researchers extend their observation capabilities in ways similar to those in other disciplines. Teachers use tools (tests etc.) to extend their observation capabilities as well. They also use statistical measures (e.g., grades) to compare teaching results. But researchers carry out these procedures more systematically, allowing for more far-reaching and reliable judgments than those normally made by teachers.

The following demonstrates a sophisticated method for conducting experimental studies that can be carried out easily by music teachers who want to be their own researchers.

A Convergence Design for Research

The principal tool that allows researchers to make controlled observations is research *design*: the arrangement of variables, test instruments, and time and environmental constraints for carrying out the study. Research design is an exercise in logic; it attempts to control the investigation such that the outcome *(effect)* can be attributed to only one explanation *(cause)*. There are many valid designs. I will introduce only one of them here, a 'convergence design'.

The convergence design is an approach that allows us to 'converge' on the specific contribution made by a variable (the one we select for manipulation) to the complete teaching situation (see Campbell & Heller, 1979). Specifically, the design answers two questions: (a) is this variable *necessary* for achieving the observed effect? and (b) is this variable *sufficient* for achieving the observed effect? The following shows how the design works.

One way of analysing a teaching situation is to consider the total set of teaching materials and strategies as a 'package'. The individual components that make up this package are called *independent* variables. For example, imagine that a music teacher called Hector is in charge of an instrumental music course for beginners that includes the following independent variables (some of these components are intentionally absurd – you will see the reason why I have included them shortly):

Musical instruments (one for each student)
Mouthpieces (one for each instrument)

Harold E. Fiske

Method books (one for each student)
Computer program to assist music reading
Kodaly handsigns

Figure 1 illustrates what we have done so far. The top
half of the diagram represents the complete package; the
bottom half shows the separation of the five different

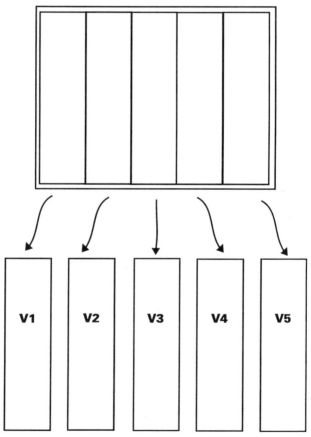

Figure 1 *The complete teaching 'package' (above) divided into five components
or variables (below).*

variables. The convergence design focuses on one of these variables (the choice is up to the teacher-researcher) and manipulates it in order to determine, first, whether it is necessary to include the variable in the package (i.e., whether the particular component is contributing to the learning effect) and, second, whether the variable is sufficient by itself (i.e., without any of the remaining variables in the package) for attaining the learning effect. Therefore, we have two *hypotheses* (or, for now, statements) about a certain variable in our teaching package, one concerning the necessity of the variable and the second concerning its sufficiency.

The convergence design requires three groups of *subjects*. ('Subjects' are those who will participate in the experiment, in this case the students enrolled in Hector's instrumental course.) These groups are designated *control* and *experimental* as follows. One group of subjects is involved in the entire teaching package. We will call this the *Package Control Group*. A second group of subjects is involved with all components of the package except the one isolated variable being manipulated. We will call this the *Package minus Component Group* (or Package minus C). This is *experimental group 1*. A third group of subjects is involved *only* with the isolated variable. We will call this the *Component minus the Package Group* (or C minus Package). This is *experimental group 2*.

In the examples that follow I will use Hector's five-component instrumental teaching package (as listed above). Each example is a test of the necessity/sufficiency hypotheses. The first two examples are intentionally absurd, illustrating the purpose of the convergence design. The third is a serious example, and we will spend more time with it.

Absurd example 1.

Suppose that Hector wants to determine the effectiveness of mouthpieces on instrumental tone quality. In this example mouthpiece is the independent (causal) variable, the one we will manipulate and the dependent (outcome) variable is tone quality production.

Hector forms the required three groups of subjects (each is a different class, all members of which are enrolled in Hector's instrumental course): (a) a Package Control Group that is involved with all five components of the package, (b) a Package minus C experimental group that is involved with all components of the teaching package except the mouthpiece component; that is, this group of students will learn to play their instruments without using a mouthpiece, and (c) a C minus Package experimental group that is involved only with the isolated independent variable, the mouthpiece; that is, this group will participate in a class in which the only thing going on is performance on a mouthpiece (i.e., no instrument, no method book, no music reading computer program, no Kodaly handsigns – see above comment regarding absurdity). Condition (b) is our test for necessity (of the mouthpiece) and condition (c) is our test for sufficiency (of the mouthpiece).

Assume that the three classes meet separately and that the groups do not interact in any way. Following six months of instruction, a Tone Quality Test is given to all of the students that allows numerical grading of each student's instrumental tone quality production (the dependent variable). It is obvious, of course, what the effect of these conditions on tone quality will be. Assume for condition (a) (the Package Control group) that the tone quality results are those normally found for beginning instrumental students. We will call the results of *any* Package Control Group 'high'. Used this way 'high' is a definition. So, using this definition, we will declare that the tone quality results of our Package Control Group are 'high' (no matter what the level of those results may actually be).

The Package Control Group results are compared against the remaining two experimental groups. This is shown in Figure 2. In this example we can assume that, for the first experimental group (Package minus C, the test for necessity), the tone quality of this group will be

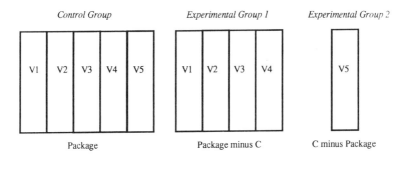

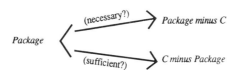

Figure 2 *Research design for the convergence approach: (a) three groups of subjects where (b) the test scores from the Package Control Group are compared against the scores from the Package minus C experimental group as a test for the necessity of the independent variable and against the scores from the C minus Package experimental group as a test of the variable's sufficiency.*

inferior to that of the Package Control Group. We will define this group's tested tone quality as 'low' (i.e., low in comparison with the Package Control Group's 'high' score). That is, we see that the tone quality of the Package minus C subjects suffers when they learn to play their instruments without a mouthpiece. Therefore, we conclude that a mouthpiece is *necessary* in order to produce tone quality equivalent (or better) to that of the Package Control Group conditions.

We can also assume for this example that tone quality produced by the mouthpiece alone (the second experimental group, C minus Package) will also be inferior (again defined as 'low') in comparison with the Package Control. That is, the mouthpiece alone is not enough to produce tone quality equivalent to (or better than) the control subjects. Therefore, we will conclude that the mouthpiece alone is *not sufficient* for producing equivalent tone quality.

Table 1 shows the four possible sets of conclusions that can be drawn from this design. The table is entered by finding the row that lists the pair of results (either 'high' or 'low') found for the two comparisons. For our absurd example 1 the combination was 'low' and 'low' for Package minus C and C minus Package respectively, confirming our conclusion that a mouthpiece is necessary but not sufficient for producing tone quality equivalent to that of the Package Control Group.

In this example we really already knew, of course, what the conclusion was prior to conducting the study. We knew it through our experience with musical instruments. The following example shows that knowing the conclusion ahead of time is not always the case.

Table 1 *Combinations of necessity and sufficiency.*

Possible Outcomes		Experimental Group 1 Package minus C	Experimental Group 2 C minus Package	Conclusion
H	H	H	H	Not necessary, but sufficient
H	L	H	L	Not necessary, not sufficient
L	H	L	H	Necessary and sufficient
L	L	L	L	Necessary, but not sufficient

where: H = 'high' score as compared with Package Control Group
L = 'low' score as compared with Package Control Group

Half-absurd Example 2.

Suppose Hector decides to test another of his variables, this time Kodaly handsigns as a means of achieving pitch and note accuracy in instrumental performance. In this study the independent variable is Kodaly handsigns and the dependent variable is pitch and note accuracy. Assume that the same three classes of students are participating in this study. Also assume that the Package Control Group includes the same five components as before. In this study the Package minus C experimental group encounter all of the components of the Package except the Kodaly handsigns. This again is a test for the necessity of the independent variable. The C minus Package experimental group encounters only the Kodaly handsigns and none of the remaining variables. This again is a test for the sufficiency of the independent variable. The latter

65

comparison is the reason this example is also absurd. But we can take advantage of this absurdity. We know that the C minus Package experimental group, the class that is taught Kodaly handsigns exclusively (none of the remaining components of the Package, including instruments or mouthpieces, are encountered) will not be able to demonstrate pitch/note accuracy in instrumental performance since they have not been taught how to play the instruments! We do not have to conduct this part of the experiment since we already know that the pitch/note accuracy scores for the C minus Package subjects will be low in comparison to the scores of the Package Control subjects. That is, whatever score the C minus Package experimental group delivers we know that it will be lower than the control group's score. Therefore, we know *a priori* that handsigns alone are *not sufficient* for producing pitch/note accuracy in instrumental performance. We will call such situations, those where we know beforehand that the scores for an experimental group will be low in comparison to the control group, the *zero option*. For zero option situations we may merely declare the comparison low without having to run that part of the experiment.

But, are Kodaly handsigns *necessary* for producing pitch/note accuracy as compared with the total teaching package encountered by the Package Control Group? Now the example is no longer absurd because we do not know the answer to that question without actually testing it formally. We might have some suspicion about the contribution of handsigns to the teaching package, but we cannot *know* what that contribution is until we test it with the control group and the single Package minus C experimental group.

Serious Example 3.

The components of Hector's teaching package included a music reading computer program. Hector wants to know whether the computer program is necessary and/or sufficient for teaching his instrumental music students to read music. So Hector prepares an experiment where the computer program is the independent variable and music reading ability is the dependent variable.

Hector assigns one of his three classes to the Package Control Group. This group receives the complete teaching package (identical to the previous examples) including the computer program. A second class is assigned to the Package minus C experimental group. The students in this group participate in the complete package except that they are not permitted to use the computer program. Instead, their only instruction in music reading will be through the method book. As before, this is our test for necessity. The third class is assigned to the C minus Package experimental group. This group experiences the computer music reading program only. (The subjects in this group do not actually learn to play an instrument.) As before, this is the our test for sufficiency.

Hector carries out his study for eight weeks, following which he administers a music reading test to all of his students in each of the three groups. Table 2 lists these (fictitious) results. Each number represents one test score. (There are 26 subjects in each of the three groups.) The following are the steps Hector follows in order to test the necessity and sufficiency of the music reading computer program.

Step 1. For each group of subjects, rank order the test scores from low to high (or high to low, if you prefer).

Step 2. For the Package Control Group *only*, find the middle score or, if you have an even number of scores, the mid-point (average) between the two middle scores. Write it out and circle it. This is called the *median*.[1]

Step 3. For the Package Control Group, count the number of subjects who scored higher than the median and the number of subjects who scored below it. (The number should be the same in both cases.) Write these numbers down as shown in Table 2.[2]

Step 4. Now examine the Package minus C Group and divide the group in two using the median from the Package Control Group as shown in Table 2. That is, use *the same value* found for the control group's median to divide the Package minus C Group. (If this score does not appear in the experimental group, divide this group at the point where this value would have been found if it had actually occurred.) [3]

Step 5. For the Package minus C Group, count the number of test scores that fall above and below the division created by step 4 (see Table 2).

Step 6. Repeat the procedures described in steps 4 and 5 for the second experimental group C minus Package (see Table 2).

If Hector is interested *only* in the effect of the music reading computer program on *this* year's group of students, then he can now make his necessary/sufficient decisions. To do so, he needs to determine whether the number of scores that fall above and below the divisions made in the control group is different from those for each of the experimental groups (i.e., the results of step 2 compared with steps 4, 5, and 6). He needs to determine whether a shift in the distribution of the scores occurred

Table 2 *Test scores from three (fictitious) groups of subjects.*

Package Control	Package minus C	C minus Package
20 ⎫	10 ⎫	10 ⎫
20	10	10
20	10	15
25	20	15
25	20	15
30	25	20
35 ⎬ 13 scores	30	20
35	30 ⎬ 15 scores	20
40	35	20
40	35	20 ⎬ 20 scores
40	35	25
40	40	25
45 ⎭	40	25
—	40	30
— Median (= 47.5)	40 ⎭	30
50 ⎫	—	30
50	—	30
50	50 ⎫	35
55	55	35
55	55	40 ⎭
60	60	—
65 ⎬ 13 scores	60 ⎬ 11 scores	—
65	65	50 ⎫
65	70	50
70	70	55 ⎬ 6 scores
80	75	55
80	85	60
85 ⎭	90 ⎭	60 ⎭

between the control and experimental conditions. If a shift did not occur (i.e., if there is no difference between the distribution of scores), then we say that the experimental scores remained 'high' (thereby invoking our criterion definition from above); if there is a difference in the distribution then we say that the experimental scores were 'low' in comparison with the control group.[4] Table 2 is then entered using the observed 'high'/ 'low' results in order to make the final conclusions regarding necessity and/or sufficiency.

In this example Hector notes that a shift has occurred: only eleven scores in the experimental group fell above the division while fifteen scores fell below it. The Package minus C test scores are lower than those of the control group. Therefore, removing the music reading program from the remaining components of the teaching package appears to result in a shift towards a greater number of lower test scores. The music reading program is judged to be 'necessary' (from Table 2) for this particular group of students. Further, the C minus Package Group scores are also lower (six scores above the division and twenty below it). Therefore, removing the remaining components of the teaching package from the music reading component appears to result in a shift to a greater number of lower scores. The music reading program is judged 'not sufficient' alone for teaching music reading to this particular group of students.

We emphasized above that Hector's conclusion is acceptable so long as he is interested only in the progress of *these particular students*. If that is all Hector is interested in, then the study is completed. But what if Hector wanted to know the effect of the music reading computer program on next year's students or other similar groups of students? Can he use these results to make a prediction about future groups of students? The answer is 'maybe, but not yet', not until he has conducted some additional statistical analyses. The observed shifts in scores are true for the subjects tested but may or may not be true of other groups of students who might encounter the same teaching package. The following will help to clarify this problem.

Using Test Scores to Make Predictions

Hector could, if he wanted to, accept his conclusion and hope that the same or similar results would occur in the future. But, a stronger approach would be to subject the test scores to *inferential statistical testing*, statistical procedures that allow us to make inferences about the behaviour of other students on the basis of the measured behaviour of current students. Some of these procedures are complex, others are quite simple. The following describes a simple one.

Introduction to Null Hypothesis Testing.

Inferential statistics is an application of inductive reasoning: drawing a conclusion from a set of *sample* observations and generalizing that conclusion to the *population* from which that sample was drawn. If we can assume that Hector's subjects are representative of his future students, then the (overall) effect of the computer music reading program on the (sample) subjects actually tested will *probably* be similar for future students (providing everything remains more or less constant). Note the emphasis on 'probably'. The statistics cannot tell us what will happen, but they can guide us to make a well-reasoned guess with some degree of confidence. Here is how.

Imagine going to a store and purchasing a bucket that contains 9000 cards, all the same size. On each of the cards is printed a number, either 1, 2, 3, 4, 5, 6, 7, 8 or 9. Assume that there is an equal number of cards showing each of the numbers. A label on the bucket assures us that the average value of the printed numbers (when they are all added together and divided by 9000) equals 5. Call this bucket, Bucket A. Imagine further that we purchase a second bucket just like it (i.e., it too contains 9000 cards, each printed with a number ranging from 1 to 9 with an average of 5, all numbers equivalently represented). Call this bucket, Bucket B. So now we have two identical buckets with identical *populations* of numbers.

Refer to Figure 3. If we draw a *sample* of, say, twenty cards at random from Bucket A, we might assume that this sample is a reasonable representation of the Bucket A *population*. The mean (or average) of this sample (and other statistics) provides an *estimate* of the mean (and other statistical descriptors) of Bucket A. Imagine that the mean of this sample is found to be 4. We know that the average of Bucket A is really 5 (the label on the bucket told us this), but we also know that sampling procedures hold no guarantee of deriving the population mean from a sample mean. The sample merely estimates the true description of the population. The difference between the true average of the population (5 in this case) and the average of a particular sample (4) is called *sampling error* (error due to our sample failing to truly reflect the parameters of the population).

Imagine now that we draw a sample of twenty cards from Bucket B and calculate *its* average. Since all of the conditions are the same as for Bucket A we have every right to expect again that sample B is a reasonable estimate of the parameters of Bucket B. Suppose that the sample B average is 6. Again we have sampling error. (We know this only because we happen to know the true average of Buckets A and B.) We can subtract the average of sample B (6) from the average of sample A (4). We know that the difference between the true average of Bucket A (5) and Bucket B (5) is zero ($5 - 5 = 0$). But the difference between our samples is -2. We will call this difference a *sampling difference* (sampling error now

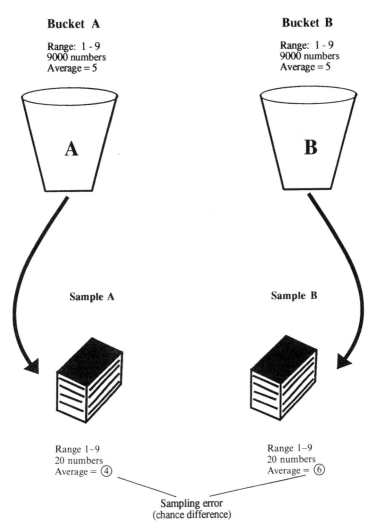

Figure 3 *Samples drawn from two or more identical populations are likely to result in differences due to sampling procedures.*

applied to the estimated difference between the true averages of Buckets A and B).

Suppose that we write this sampling difference down on paper, toss the cards back into their respective buckets, thoroughly mix and stir the cards up, and draw two more samples of twenty cards each, one from Bucket A and the second from Bucket B. We then calculate their averages and the sampling difference, write this difference down on the paper, return the cards to their buckets, stir them up, and draw two more samples again. Imagine that we repeat this procedure some large number of times, say five or ten thousand. If we did so, we would record five or ten thousand sample differences.

Now, we can take this record of sample differences, rank order them from low to high (in respect to their positive or negative sign) and plot their frequencies (i.e., show on a graph the number of times each of the mean differences occurred). The result will be a 'normally distributed' curve of mean differences (see Figure 4). The average (mean) of these numbers (i.e., the average of the sampling differences) is an estimate of the true difference between Buckets A and B.

Now, here is where Hector's study comes in. A research study uses real people data and not artificial bucket data. And, instead of taking large numbers of samples as we did with our bucket example, an experimental study usually takes only *one* sample (per subject group). The single sample of data is then used as if it were yet one more sample of bucket data (rather than the people data that they really are) in order to determine the probability that the sample could have been obtained by chance alone.

Hector's students represent *one sample* from a poten-

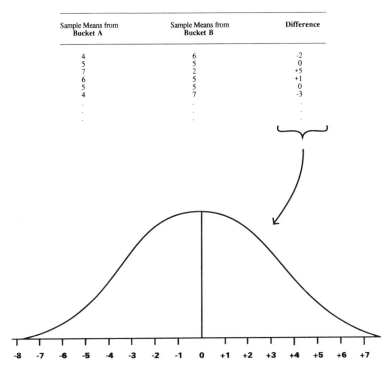

Sample Means from Bucket A	Sample Means from Bucket B	Difference
4	6	-2
5	5	0
7	2	+5
6	5	+1
5	5	0
4	7	-3
.	.	.
.	.	.
.	.	.

-8 -7 -6 -5 -4 -3 -2 -1 0 +1 +2 +3 +4 +5 +6 +7

Figure 4 *Plotting individual sample mean (average) differences results in a normally distributed curve of mean differences (or curve of average differences).*

tially large *population*, all of the students who will ever participate in the school's instrumental music programme either now or in the future. Hector's students were assigned (assume randomly) to three different sections, designated 'Package Control', 'Package minus C experimental group', and 'C minus Package experimental group' (see Figure 5). Each group received different teaching conditions (as described earlier) following which a test was given to all the students. The resulting test scores are data (observations) reflecting each subject's music reading ability following participation in the study. This takes us

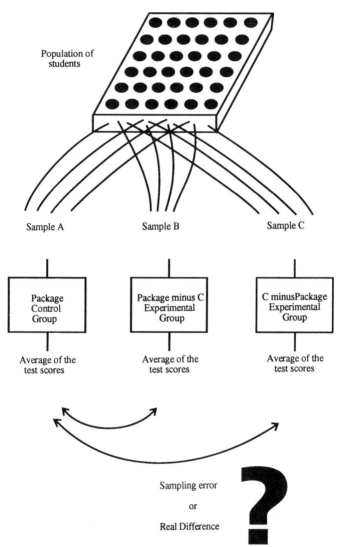

Figure 5 *Subjects are randomly drawn from a defined population and assigned to either the control group or one of the experimental groups. (This figure is analogous to Figure 3.)*

up to where we left off: Hector discovered that shifts in the scores occurred between the control and each of the experimental groups. But does this shift represent a *real* difference or a *chance* difference? The shift is, of course, a 'real' representation of the students who were tested. But the question concerns the likelihood of observing the same kind of shift with future samples. How large a difference (how much of a shift) between the samples is required before we decide that the difference is real, that it is *caused* by the manipulated (independent) variable and not merely a difference likely to be found by chance alone?

Statistical tests determine the probability that the observed results could have been found by chance alone (as if we were dealing with bucket data rather than real people data). A statistical test is a test of a *null hypothesis.* For the convergence design there are two null hypotheses, one about necessity and the other about sufficiency. The wording of these hypotheses is:

1. There is *no difference* between the distribution of 'high' and 'low' scores for the Package Control Group and the Package minus C experimental group. (This is a re-wording of our original test for necessity.)
2. There is *no difference* between the distribution of 'high' and 'low' scores for the Package Control Group and the C minus Package experimental group. (This is a re-wording of our original test for sufficiency.)

In short, the statistical comparison begins from a point of neutrality: 'there is no difference between......' We let the results of the statistical measures show us, objectively, the probability to which the observed difference in score distributions can be found by chance alone. There are

77

many tests available for doing this, each designed in respect to the circumstances of the experimental situation (e.g., number of dependent and independent variables, type of data, size of sample, and others). The test we will use in our example is a version of the chi square test. ('Chi', the twenty-second letter of the Greek alphabet, is pronounced 'ki' as in the word 'kite'.)

Here are the steps involved in completing chi square. They continue on from the earlier list and are very easy! (Refer to Figure 6.)

Step 7. We will test the necessity hypothesis first. Write down the number of 'high' and 'low' test scores for both the Package Control and the Package minus C experimental group (the same 'high' and 'low' scores found in steps 3, 4 and 5) in the boxes of the table as shown in Figure 6.

Step 8. Next, total separately boxes A + B; C + D; A + C; and B + D (as shown in Figure 6). Then calculate the grand total, boxes A + B + C + D.

Step 9. Multiply the figures in the boxes as follows: A × D and B × C. Write down the answers to these.

Step 10. Substitute the results from steps 8 and 9 in the following formula:

$$\chi^2 = \frac{N\left[(AD - BC) - \dfrac{N}{2}\right]^2}{(A + B)(C + D)(A + C)(B + D)}$$

If BC is larger than AD, then reverse the order of these in this part of the equation: i.e., BC − AD.

Step 11. Solve the equation. The result is the chi square value.

Step 12. Interpret the chi square value found in step 11

by checking it against the table of critical values shown in Figure 6. This step requires a short explanation.

Chi square values (and most other inferential statistical test values) show us where on the curve of mean differences the particular sample comparison would fall *if this comparison were comprised of sample (bucket) data.* That is, the data are treated as if they came from populations where the difference between those populations is known to be zero (as with Buckets A and B). The comparison is made as if our real people data were really bucket data and this was yet one more round of selecting two samples, calculating their averages, calculating their mean differences, etc. In short, what we determine is the probability that the difference between the real people samples (Package Control and Package minus C) could be found by chance alone if it were known beforehand (as in the case of the bucket data) that the difference is due to random (selection) error. Fortunately, statisticians have done the hard work for us. (They have, in a sense, drawn the millions of samples required to construct the curve of mean differences.) All we have to do is to compare our computed chi square value against a table of chi square values where this probability of occurrence is shown (i.e., our table of critical values).

Now, how much of a risk should we take? How do we know whether we should we accept the null hypothesis or reject it? We know that differences found in our bucket sample comparisons are *always due to chance* no matter how large a difference is found. It is possible that our real people data comparisons are also due to chance. The independent sample may not *really* be having an effect; the difference may again be due to random error. But it may not be. The difference may be a *real* difference. The

	High	Low	Total
Package	**A** 13	**B** 13	26
Package minus C	**C** 11	**D** 15	26
	24	28	52

$$\chi^2 = \frac{N\left[(AD - BC) - \dfrac{N}{2}\right]^2}{(A + B)(C + D)(A + C)(B + D)}$$

$$= \frac{52\left[(195 - 143) - \dfrac{52}{2}\right]^2}{(26)(26)(24)(28)}$$

$$= \frac{35152}{454272}$$

= .077 (Not statistically significant;

therefore 'high', therefore *Not Necessary*)

	High	Low	Total
Package	**A** 13	**B** 13	26
C minus Package	**C** 6	**D** 20	26
	19	33	52

$$\chi^2 = \frac{N\left[(AD - BC) - \dfrac{N}{2}\right]^2}{(A + B)(C + D)(A + C)(B + D)}$$

$$= \frac{52\left[(260 - 78) - \dfrac{52}{2}\right]^2}{(26)(26)(19)(33)}$$

$$= \frac{1265472}{423852}$$

= 2.99 (Statistically significant;

therefore 'low', therefore *Not Sufficient*)

Figure 6 *Chi Square calculation and interpretation.*

independent variable may be having a genuine effect. So, knowing that the mean difference between our real people samples could be found by chance alone, at what level of probability are we willing to say 'I'll bet our observed difference is not really due to chance after all because the probability of finding this difference by chance alone is so small?'

There is no absolute answer to this question. Which ever way we choose will always involve a risk that we have made the wrong decision about the null hypothesis (i.e., accepting rather than rejecting it; rejecting rather than accepting it). Traditionally, most researchers choose what is called the *.05 significance level*. That is, if our chi square value tells us that the difference could be found by chance alone only five times out of 100 or less, then we are normally willing to take that chance and declare the null hypothesis *rejected*; if greater than .05 we normally declare the null hypothesis *accepted*. We make our decision by comparing our obtained chi square value against the Table of Critical Values (see Table 3): in order to reject the null hypothesis the chi square value must be

Table 3 *Table of critical values.*

Chi Square value	Significance level
2.71	.05
3.84	.025
5.41	.01
6.64	.001

The Chi Square value shown in Table 3 is the minimum value that must be attained in order to reject the null hypothesis at the given significance level. (Refer to example: the value .077 that was found ie less than 2.71, therefore the null hypothesis was excepted; the value that was found in the second part of the analysis, 2.99, is greater than the minimum value, 2.71, but less than the next value shown, 3.84, so the null hypothesis was rejected at the .05 significance level.)

equal to or exceed the value associated with the given probability level; if not, the null hypothesis is accepted.

Step 13. Once we have tested our null hypothesis about necessity we carry out the same procedures for testing our null hypothesis about sufficiency, this time using the scores for the remaining experimental group.

One final detail of terminology: when we reject a null hypothesis we say that the difference between the (distribution of) scores of the experimental and control groups is *statistically significant*. When we decide to accept the null hypothesis (some researchers call this 'failure to reject the null hypothesis') we simply say that the difference is not statistically significant. (Attaching the word 'statistically' to the word 'significant' is a requirement. Significance here does *not* mean 'important', as in 'the observed difference is an important difference'; the difference is significant merely in the sense of the probability that it is not a chance difference. You must use your own criteria to decide whether the size of the difference is important or not.)

In our example, the chi square value found in the first test was .077, less than the required critical value of 2.71 (see Table 3). Therefore, we accepted the null hypothesis, concluding that the scores for the Package minus C Group remained 'high' in comparison with the Package Control Group. That is, the difference was not statistically significant. In the second test, the chi square value was 2.99, which is greater than the required critical value of 2.71. Therefore, we rejected the null hypothesis, concluding that the scores for the C minus Package Group were 'low' in comparison with the Package Control Group. That is, the difference was statistically significant. A 'high' score result for necessity and a 'low' score result for sufficiency leads to the final conclusion that our (fictitious) music reading computer program is neither necessary nor sufficient for affecting music reading, at least in respect to the teaching package as a whole.

Why We Go Through All of This

1.   Formal experimental procedures allow us to compare conditions with greater precision and objectivity than can normally be measured informally.
2.   These procedures allow us to analyse our teaching strategies and materials, and to make predictions about their effect on future students.
3.   Experimental studies carry more weight than informal studies, particularly with school administrators and funding organizations.
4.   Experimental research procedures teach us to think more logically and systematically.
5.   Experimental research is fun.

Recommended Reading

Barnes, S. H. (1982). *A Cross-Section of Research in Music Education*. Washington, D.C.: University Press of America. Contains 22 previously published examples of music education research studies, each employing a different methodology.

Campbell, W. C. and Heller, J. J. (1979). Convergence Procedures for Investigating Music Listening Tasks. *Council for Research in Music Education,* 59, 18–23. An excellent example of the convergence design. This article is the inspiration behind the present chapter.

Campbell, D. T. and Stanley, J. C. (1963). *Experimental and Quasi-Experimental Designs for Research*. Chicago: Rand McNally. A classic text concerning the theory and practice of research design.

Cook, T. D. and Campbell, D. T. (1979). *Quasi-Experimentation: Design and Analysis Issues for Field Settings.* Chicago: Rand McNally. Expands on the theory of cause and effect, and provides additional examples of quasi-experimental designs beyond those discussed in Cambell and Stanley (1963).

Colwell, R. (ed.) (1992). *Handbook for Research in Music Teaching and Learning*. New York: Schirmer. A comprehensive collection of literature reviews by various authors concerning many of the research areas that are of interest to music education.

Council for Research in Music Education Bulletin. University of Illinois. One of the principal music education research journals; features research reports, reviews of the literature, and thesis critiques. Four issues per year.

Heller, J. and Campbell, W. (1985). Response: View from the Fourth Estate. *Council for Research in Music Education Bulletin*, 83, 27–31. A critical appraisal of the state of research in music education.

Journal of Research in Music Education. Music Educators National Conference, Reston, Virginia. One of the principal music education research journals; provides research reports. Four issues per year.

Madsen, C. K. and Madsen, C. H. (1970). *Experimental Research in Music*. Englewood Cliffs. N.J.: Prentice-Hall. A fine introduction to music education research theory and methodology.

Popham, W. J. and Sirotnik, K. A. (1973). *Educational Statistics: Use and Interpretation* (second edition). New York: Harper and Row. Dated, but still an excellent introduction to experimental research methodology.

Rainbow, E. L. and Froehlich, H. C. (1987). *Research in Music Education: An Introduction of Systematic Inquiry*. New York: Schirmer Books. A good introductory text to research methodology.

Radocy, R. E. and Boyle, J. D. (1988). *Psychological Foundations of Musical Behavior (second edition)*. Springfield, Illinois: Charles C. Thomas. An excellent summary and discussion of some major music education research interests.

Notes

1. Note that the median is not the same statistic as the mean; the mean is the average of all the test scores of any one group (or of all the groups).
2. Sometimes the median score will be achieved by more than one subject. In these cases, you should still divide the subjects equally so that the same number of subjects continue to score above and below this division. You should do this even though the score that actually represents the 'median' is, for these cases, achieved by subjects on both sides of the divider.
3. If multiple occurrences of the median's value are found in the experimental group, divide these particular scores evenly, assigning half to the 'above-the-median' scores and the remaining half to the 'below-the-median' scores.

4. Normally a shift to lower scores will be the case. It is possible, however, that a shift towards higher scores will be found if, for the Package versus Package minus C comparison, the independent variable is for some reason inhibiting the remaining components of the teaching package or, for the Package versus C minus Package comparison, the remaining components of the teaching package are inhibiting the effect of the independent variable. The proper interpretation in both cases would be 'higher' followed by the usual interpretation offered by Table 1 and additional research concerning why the inhibiting occurred

References

Campbell, W. C. and Heller, J. J. (1979). Convergence Procedures for Investigating Music Listening Tasks. *Council for Research in Music Education Bulletin,* 59, 18–23.

Heller, J. and Campbell, W. (1985). Response: View from the Fourth Estate. *Council for Research in Music Education Bulletin,* 83, 27–31.

Strawson, P. F. (1952) *Introduction to Logical Theory.* London: Methuen.

5

Observational Research

CORNELIA YARBROUGH

Musical behaviours are often taken for granted in our preoccupation with a written musical score. Somehow it seems more important to analyse the chord structure and rhythmic accents, to develop a musical understanding or idea of what the composer intended, and to place all of this in historical perspective than to analyse how we translate these musical ideas into musical behaviours. As we consider all aspects of a musical score, of musical historiography, of philosophical pronouncements regarding the art of music, we may also stretch our thinking toward an actualization or realization of these ideas. How have musicians translated these ideas into musical behaviours? If music is an active as opposed to passive art, how might we analyse that activity? How might we describe our musical interactions with musical elements?

Observational research methodology is used in music research when the researcher's purpose is to describe the current conditions concerning the musical nature of a group of persons, a number of music objects, or a class of musical events. This chapter will examine the use of systematic observational techniques to describe musical behaviours or events.

Observational research in music describes what is presently occurring. It may involve the definition, recording, analysis, and interpretations of the present nature, make up, or processes of musical phenomena. The focus is, therefore, on prevailing conditions in music or musical situations or on how a person or group behaves in a musical situation.

In the fields of music education and music therapy, practitioners and researchers alike are concerned with two general aspects of behaviour: attention to a stimulus (i.e., music) and a response to it (i.e., composing, performing, listening, verbalizing, conceptualizing, using music for extra-musical purposes). It would seem that those music teachers and conductors who are most successful in maintaining attentive classes or performing groups, eliciting high levels of achievement or performance, and establishing favourable attitudes toward music, have several observable characteristics in common. First, they are usually highly approving. Second, they dispense approval and disapproval in a very dramatic way by maintaining eye contact, using body movement and contrasting facial expressions, and conducting in an expressive way. Finally, they are efficient users of class and rehearsal time.

Through systematic observation of music classes and rehearsals, one may begin to understand the relationship between these characteristics of teacher and conductor behaviour and student attentiveness, performance, and attitude. For example, did the altos miss that entry because the conductor did not maintain eye contact, use an expressive left hand gesture, and lean towards them? Were students in that kindergarten class off-task because the music teacher failed to reinforce appropriately? Did that junior high school band stay 95% on-task because the conductor was highly approving, kept the rehearsal moving at a rapid pace by changing the activity often, and used dramatic overt behaviour?

Controlled observation has been used as a technique

to determine patterns of instruction in music rehearsals. Verbatim typescripts of 79 experienced and inexperienced music teachers were analysed. Categories of teacher and student behaviour developed and defined from prior research formed the basis for this analysis. Sequenced patterns of teaching labelled direct instruction in previous research were observed and counted. Results indicated that experienced teachers use more time in giving directions concerning who is to play and where they are to begin and less time in giving musical information. When observation categories and techniques regarding sequential patterns are solidified in terms of validity and reliability, experimental techniques can be used to isolate the effects of the various patterns on the musical behaviour of students (Yarbrough & Price, 1981).

Another more technically controlled observation technique has involved EEG technology to observe the brain waves of musicians and non-musicians while listening to music. Wagner found that musicians produce more alpha brain waves than non-musicians while listening to music. This result was most interesting because alpha brain waves are of a relatively low frequency and are associated with states of transcendental meditation. It had been hypothesized that musicians would produce more beta brain waves since they would be more attentive and therefore would be processing what they were listening to in a more informed manner than non-musicians. However, this was not the case. Instead, musicians produced more alpha brainwaves. This result has raised many questions regarding the function of the brain while listening to music (Wagner, 1975).

Thus, research using systematic observation methodology has begun to define music teaching and learning behaviours, develop instrumentation for measuring those behaviours, and enable the study of relationships among them. The next section of this chapter includes a description of the basic techniques of the methodology and the kinds of research questions the methodology may best address. In addition, studies using the methodology and future directions for observational research in music will be discussed.

Operational Definitions

The first step in the systematic observation of music behaviour is to define operationally, or pin-point, the behaviour(s) to be measured. This demands isolating behaviours which can be observed, and measuring these behaviours with high reliability. Behaviours must be defined such that others can read the definition, observe the behaviour simultaneously with a second observer, and record the same thing. This requires specific examples of the behaviours to be observed. For instance, if the behaviour to be observed is eye contact, we might define it as

> Looking at the entire group, section, individuals within the group, the music, or something other than the group section, or individuals within the group (e.g., ceiling, floor) for at least three continuous seconds. No eye contact occurs when the teacher maintains it for less than three continuous seconds.

It should be noted that value determinations, whether different types of eye contact are good or bad, are not a part of the operational definition.

Other examples of operational definitions of musical behaviours are those developed for magnitude of conductor behaviour (Yarbrough, 1975). Here, magnitude was defined as 'intensity of reinforcement'. Drawing from behavioural literature outside the field of music allowed further expansion of the definition to include the characteristics of (a) dramatic change of pace, (b) dynamic presentation of materials, and (c) direct, personal delivery of reinforcement in order to affect student performance (O'Leary & Becker, 1968–1969; O'Leary, Kaufman, Kass, & Drabman, 1970). Transferring these ideas to conductor behaviour resulted in the following operational definitions of magnitude of conductor behaviour (Yarbrough, 1975, p. 138; see Figure 1).

Thus, observational methodology begins with the development of specific, detailed definitions of behaviours which singularly or in combination represent a musical and instructional concept. Once these operational definitions have been developed, one must carefully consider the measurement technique which will be used before an observation tool can be designed.

Therefore, the second step in systematic observation methodology relates to the choice of methods for making written records. These methods include: counting, time sampling, automatic recording, and continuous recording. Figure 2 has been adapted from a similar figure in Hall and Van Houten (1983) with transfers to specified music behaviours. It shows the methods of recording, examples of behaviours which might be recorded by that method, and the pros and cons of the method.

Counting Behaviour

When there are only two or three behaviours to be observed, simply counting them would seem to be the most efficient way to proceed. This is most often the case

Teacher Behaviour	High Magnitude	Low Magnitude
Eye Contact	Maintains with group and/or individuals throughout rehearsal.	Never looks at individuals or group. Looks at music, ceiling, or in direction of piano.
Closeness	Frequently walks or leans toward chorus or particular section	Stands behind the music stand at all times. Music stand is always a minimum of four feet from chorus.
Volume and Modulation of Voice	Volume constantly varies. Wide range of volume as well as speaking pitch. Voice reflects enthusiasm and vitality.	Volume remains clearly audible but the same approximate volume and pitch throughout rehearsal. Voice reflects little enthusiasm and vitality.
Gestures	Uses arms and hands to aid in musical phrasing. Great variety of movement. Varies size of conducting patterns to indicate phrases, dynamics, and the like.	Strict conducting pattern, never varying. Uses arms and hands for attacks and releases. Exact movements.
Facial Expressions	Face reflects sharp contrasts between approval/disapproval Approval is expressed by grinning, laughing aloud, raising eyebrows, widening eyes. Disapproval is expressed by frowning, knitting brow, pursing lips, narrowing eyes.	Neutral mask. No frowns. No smiles.
Rehearsal Pace	Rapid and exciting. Quick instructions. Minimal talking. Less than one second between activity. Frequently gives instructions to group while they are singing.	Slow and methodical. Meticulous care and and detail in instructions. Always stops group to give instructions.

Figure 1 *Operational definitions of high and low magnitude.*

Recording Method	Behaviours	Pros	Cons
Counting Behaviour	Number of approvals, disapprovals, and mistakes of reinforcement.	Easy to use when definitions are specific and reliable.	Difficult to use if many behaviours are being counted.
Time Sampling	Intervals of time spent instructing and in group performance.	Does not consume much of the observer's time.	Not useful when behaviour occurs infrequently.
Automatic	Duration and dynamics of keyboard performances (computer). Time spent singing or playing in an ensemble rehearsal (time clock). Cent deviation from correct pitch (computer or tuner).	Precise. Objective. Quantitative. Gives information on how often and how long a behaviour occurs.	Expensive. Inflexible.
Continuous	Video- or audio-taped recordings of classes and/or rehearsals followed by scripting, categorizing, counting, and timing.	Many classes of behaviour can be included. Useful when operational definitions are questionable or being developed. Also, allows examination of the total situation.	Difficult and tedious. Requires observer's constant attention.
	Continuous computer analysis of music preferences	Allows pin-pointing of peak experiences as they occur while listening to music.	Complex set-up at this time, but holds much promise for the future.

Figure 2 *Recording methods in the systematic observation of music behaviour.*

in self-evaluation or music therapy case studies. Here one may want to target a few behaviours to increase or decrease. An operational definition would be developed for each behaviour. The procedure then becomes one of recording the number of behaviours counted over a period of minutes, days, weeks, or months. Subsequently, a reinforcement technique might be applied to attempt to change the number of times the behaviour occurs. During the application of the reinforcement technique, the researcher or self-evaluator would continue counting the targeted behaviours. Finally, the reinforcement technique might be withdrawn to determine whether the change in behaviours counted could be maintained in the absence of the reinforcement technique. Of importance, is the fact that counting continues throughout the self-evaluative or therapeutic study.

Numerous musical behaviours lend themselves to this technique. For example, one might count the number of rhythmic errors which occur during a performance or the number of approvals and disapprovals given by a teacher in an elementary music classroom. Music therapists might be interested in the number of times a child with cerebral palsy independently lifts his head or the number of inappropriate verbalizations of a child. Decisions regarding techniques to increase or decrease the behaviours counted, require creative thought during which the characteristics of the individual (both researcher and client) must be considered.

Time Sampling

The earliest observational research in music focused on the reinforcement component, i.e., approvals and disapprovals, in music teaching. As the concept of reinforcement was explored, researchers targeted eight different behaviours which might demonstrate that concept. These behaviours included academic approval, academic disapproval, social approval, social disapproval, and mistakes of academic or social approval or disapproval. They were then defined operationally such that two observers could independently agree upon them.

The Teacher Observation Form was then developed to count the number of approvals and disapprovals using a time sampling technique consisting of an 'observe interval' and a 'record interval' (Madsen & Madsen, 1981). This technique prescribed that the observer should observe a teacher for fifteen seconds and then record what they observed (i.e., approvals, disapprovals, and inappropriate reinforcement) for five seconds. This procedure continued for approximately 17 minutes, or the length of the observation form (Madsen & Madsen, 1981, p. 220).

Extending Madsen and Madsen's observational approaches, Choral and Instrumental Rehearsal Observation forms were designed to (a) time sample the number of approvals, disapprovals, instructional instances, group and sectional performance; and the number of students who were off-task (Madsen & Yarbrough, 1985, p. 57); and (b) sample Music Conductor behaviour such as activity (instruction, singing along with the group, teaching while the group is performing), body movement (approach, departure, stationary), conducting gestures (strict, expressive, none), eye contact (group, individual, music, other), facial expressions (approval, disapproval, neutral), speech speed (steady, hesitant, repetitive), voice pitch (low, variable, high), and voice volume (soft, normal, loud) (Madsen & Yarbrough, 1985, p.61).

Observation procedures for these forms are similar to those outlined for the Teacher Observation Form. However, for these forms, behaviour is sampled four times per minute instead of three. Therefore, the observe interval is ten seconds and the record interval is five seconds. The Music Conductor Observation Form was designed for use with videotape, thus allowing for repeated viewings.

Observation forms have also been developed for use in basic conducting technique courses. These forms enable conducting students to self-assess accuracy (recorded as +) or inaccuracy (recorded as -) of beat pattern, tempo, style, dynamics, eye contact, preparations, releases, and cueing (Madsen & Yarbrough, pp. 116–117). Basic Conducting Observation Form A may be used to evaluate time sampled conducting behaviour with a ten second observe and five second record interval or simply to count the occurrence of each specified behaviour within each measure of music conducted. Basic Conducting Observation Form B was designed to provide an opportunity to evaluate each occurrence of a preparation, release, and cue.

Automatic Recording

Automatic observation of the accuracy of the musical task presentation and student response has been accomplished using Macintosh computer systems, MIDI, an analogue to digital converter, and Performer (Mark of the Unicorn, 1989) software. Figure 3 shows MIDI data from a pitch-matching study which explored the ability of inaccurate singers to match descending minor thirds sung by male, female, and child singers. In this illustration, we see the pitches sung by the female model and the responses of an inaccurate singer to that model.

The computer data obtained (using Performer software) for two of the models is displayed in three columns (see Table 1). From left to right, the first column

95

indicates beginning time for each note sung, expressed in terms of the measure number, which beat in the measure, and the 'tick' on which the note began (480 ticks comprise a quarter note in a metronomic context); the second column expresses the pitch name of each note that was sung; and the third column represents the exact duration of each note sung in units of full beats (480 ticks) and/or fractions of beats, the first numbers representing the beats and the second number representing 'ticks'.

Table 1 *MIDI data from female and male vocal models.*

	Beginning	Pitch	Duration
Female Model:	4|1|157	F#4	0|012
Total Duration = 903 ticks	4|1|169	G4	0|109
Duration of G = 401	4|1|283	G4	0|075
Duration of E = 320	4|1|360	G#4	0|022
Percentage Correct - 79.84	4|1|384	G4	0|043
	4|1|427	G#4	0|037
	4|1|465	G4	0|053
	4|2|039	G#4	0|029
	4|2|068	G4	0|053
	4|2|121	G#4	0|030
	4|2|151	G4	0|011
	4|2|162	F#4	0|014
	4|2|177	G4	0|057
	4|2|296	F4	0|024
	4|2|320	E4	0|302
	4|3|142	F4	0|014
	4|3|159	E4	0|018
Male Model:	3|2|453	G3	0|169
Total Duration = 827 ticks	3|3|190	G3	0|035
Duration of G = 280	3|3|238	F#3	0|052
Duration of E = 363	3|3|290	G3	0|076
Percentage Correct = 77.75	3|3|421	E3	0|042
	3|4|000	E3	0|142
	3|4|144	D#3	0|036
	3|4|180	E3	0|056
	3|4|244	D#3	0|036
	3|4|280	E3	0|059
	3|4|339	D#3	0|036
	3|4|375	E3	0|043
	3|4|418	D#3	0|024
	3|4|444	E3	0|021

For purposes of this observation technique, correct and incorrect notes sung were observed in column two; durations were computed from the data in column three. To describe the correct pitch content of the data set for each model, the total duration for all pitches in each MIDI data set were summed; then the durations for all Gs and Es appearing in the correct order were summed; and finally, the G plus E durations were divided by the total duration to achieve a percentage of time during which correct pitches were sung in the correct order.

Thus, data obtained represented time spent singing correct pitches or duration of pitch accuracy. Not surprisingly, results demonstrated that inaccurate singers could more easily match the female model than the male model (Yarbrough, Green, Benson, & Bowers, 1991).

Other research, using this kind of MIDI data, has compared dynamics and articulation of keyboard performances. A measurement of dynamics is achieved by reading the MIDI data indicating the velocity of keystroke. The scale of measurement is from one to 64 with the smaller number indicating a slower velocity of keystroke resulting in a softer dynamic level, and the larger number indicating a faster velocity of keystroke resulting in a louder dynamic level. Articulation (staccato, legato, and so forth) is measured by reading the numbers representing duration. Results have shown that graduate and undergraduate piano majors can imitate a model's articulation quite well, but they have great difficulty in imitating dynamics. Research continues along these lines using children who are studying piano and comparing different teaching methods to improve performance of dynamics (Sharp, 1986; Yarbrough, Speer, & Parker, March 1990).

97

Another type of automated recording is that using a Continuous Response Digital Interface (CRDI) to a computer. Madsen and his associates in the Center for Music Research at Florida State University have pioneered the use of this device to study operant music preferences. The CRDI uses a potentiometer enclosed in a protective case and mounted into a piece of Plexiglas. The potentiometer is fitted with a knob and pointer with a guide mechanism such that it may be moved left and right on an arc of 250 degrees. The CRDI pointer is positioned above an evaluative response overlay. Thus, subjects can listen to a musical excerpt and simultaneously twist the knob moving it along a continuum from 0 (negative response) to 250 (positive response). This mechanism is further connected to an interface which translates incoming voltage from an analogue to a digital representation ranging from 0–250 degrees; that is, placement of the pointer along the dial sends a corresponding voltage which is then converted to a numerical rating. These numerical ratings are automatically recorded by computer for subsequent analysis (Madsen, 1990).

Results from Madsen's early research using the CRDI while subjects listened to a 20 minute excerpt from Act I of Puccini's *La Bohème* demonstrated that subjects' aesthetic experiences did group at certain points throughout the excerpt. These experiences were relatively short (15 seconds each) preceded by a period of concentrated focus of attention, and generally followed by an 'afterglow' ranging from 15 seconds to several minutes. All subjects reported having at least one aesthetic experience and also that movement of the dial roughly approximated their experiences. Aesthetic experiences for subjects seemed to cluster at many of the same places in the music with one collective 'peak' experience which was represented by the highest and lowest dial movements. This innovative measurement technique certainly holds much promise for future research (Madsen, Britten & Capperella-Sheldon, 1991).

Continuous Recording

Systematic observation techniques have been used in music research to isolate and define components of an adaptation of the direct instruction model for teaching. The earliest model for direct instruction defined interactive units of teaching in which the sequential order of events, or pattern of instruction, was of paramount importance. Specifically, the pattern began with the teacher's presentation of the task to be learned, followed by student interaction with the task and the teacher, and solidified by immediate praise or corrective feedback related to the task presented (Becker, Englemann, & Thomas, 1971).

As can be seen in Figure 3, sequential patterns of instruction in music have been identified, components of those patterns have been operationally defined, and subcategories of each component have been developed and defined. Thus, verbal interactions among teachers and students can now be observed and analysed (Price, 1989; Yarbrough & Price, 1981, 1989; Yarbrough, Price, & Bowers, 1991).

One of the most recent observational techniques is that of scripting entire rehearsal periods, categorizing each activity, and timing or counting each occurrence of every activity. This technique has been used extensively to study sequential patterns in teacher/student inter-

Teacher Presentations (1)

1a - academic musical task presentation (talking about musical or performance aspects, including modelling by teacher or piano and questioning)
1d - direction (giving directions regarding who will, or where to sing/play; counting beats, usually ending in 'ready, go'; questioning)
1s - social task presentation (presenting rules of behaviour)
1o - off-task statement (unnecessary and irrelevant comments such as talking to oneself)

Student Responses (2)

2p - performance (entire ensemble or sections performing)
2v - verbal (ensemble members asking or answering a question, or making a statement)
2nv - non-verbal (ensemble members nodding heads, raising hands, or moving in response to teacher instruction)

Reinforcement (3)

3a - verbal academic or social approval (positive statement about student performance or social behaviour)
3d - verbal academic or social disapproval (negative statement about student performance or social behaviour)
Specific - exact feedback containing musical information
Non-specific - vague feedback containing no musical information

Sequential Patterns:

Complete - Presentation of Task (1) - Student Response (2) - Reinforcement (3)
Correct:	1a - 2 - 3a specific
	1a - 2 - 3d specific
Incorrect:	1d - 2 - 3a specific
	1d - 2 - 3a non-specific
	1d - 2 - 3d specific
	1d - 2 - 3d non-specific
	1a - 2 - 3a non-specific
	1a - 2 - 3d non-specific

Incomplete - Presentation of Task (1) - Student Response (2)
1a - 2
1d - 2

Figure 3 *Operational definitions of sequential patterns of instruction in music.*

actions. The script contains the words spoken by the teacher and describes student responses. The idea is to create a script resembling that of a dramatic play. Additional information can then be added to the script such as the codes defined in Figure 3 and the number of seconds which each coded segment of script lasts.

Reliability

All of the observation techniques require a special technique for the measurement of observation reliability
called inter-observer agreement. This is due to the fact
that if reliable measurement procedures are not used, it
might be possible for the behaviour to remain stable while
the recording of the behaviour changes. Conversely, it
might be possible for the behaviour to change while the
record of it remains unchanged.

Inter-observer agreement provides added confidence
that it is indeed the behaviour that has changed from one
condition to another and that the behaviour has been
adequately defined. The formula used for the computation
of inter-observer agreement is the number of agreements
between two independent observers divided by the number of agreements plus disagreements. This results in a
percentage of observer agreement. Agreement of less than
70% is considered unacceptable. Should this occur,
observers may need retraining or the observation instrument may need revision. When a reliable measurement
technique has been achieved, data can be gathered concerning the occurrence of the operationally defined behav-
iour(s) over time, and the method of reporting data can
be designed.

Observational Design and Application

Although many observational research studies are purely
descriptive in nature, many also go another step by
attempting to change the behaviour which has been
observed. This requires more sophisticated knowledge of
the principles of logic, more rigorous operational defi-

nitions of variables under study, and judicious application of statistical analysis to results.

Experimental research in music using observational data as a dependent measure begins with the assumption that musical behaviour is lawful, that is, that there is a functional relationship between cause (independent variable) and effect (dependent variable). Having made this assumption, each experimental research design represents a complicated endeavour to manipulate an independent variable to test or isolate the effect of that manipulation on the dependent variable. For example, a pianist might assume that there is a functional relationship between the fingering of a particular scale passage (independent variable) and the accuracy of the performance of that scale (dependent variable). To determine if that relationship is functional he or she might manipulate the independent variable by altering the fingering of the scale. The effect of this manipulation would be determined by the accuracy of subsequent performance of the scale.

There are two methods of experimentation in music: 'behavioural' and 'statistical'. The logic of behavioural design is that of continuous measurement over time with each subject serving as his or her own control. The logic of statistical design is that of discrete measurement of samples from varied or counterbalanced time periods. Behavioural experimentation is concerned with individual changes; statistical, with group changes.

In statistical design one is concerned with the size of the sample, i.e. how many subjects are being studied. In behavioural design, the number of subjects is not so crucial since each individual case is of utmost importance. Statistical experimenters are interested in generalizing the results of experiments to larger populations; this explains their interest in a large N (number of subjects, for example). Behavioural experimenters are not interested in generalizing the results of experiments to larger populations; they believe that the behaviour of each individual or group is under unique environmental control.

Statistical analysis involves comparisons of samples. Measurements are taken on discrete entities. Subsequently, each group measurement (O) may be compared with every other group measurement using the same dependent variable. If the differences are great enough, assumptions are made about the effect of the independent variable (X).

Appropriate analysis for behavioural design generally takes the form of graphic analysis. Continuous lines connecting points illustrate a relationship between variables and a predictable as well as environmental change over intervals of time.

Music studies have in the past used behavioural and statistical methods of experimentation. Music therapists have made the chief contributions in behavioural design. Some studies employ complete reversal designs with graphic analysis and may involve either a single subject or a group of subjects (Hauck & Martin, 1970; Jorgenson, 1971; Jorgenson & Parnell, 1970; Morgan & Lindsley, 1966; Rieber, 1969; Steele, 1971). The logic of complete reversal designs is reflected in the graphic analyses of those which show the effect of baseline (that is, data collected before the independent variable is introduced), introduction of the independent variable, return to baseline (withdrawal of the independent variable), and re-introduction of the independent variable. Musicians may readily identify with the 'form' of the behavioural complete reversal design: A (baseline), B (introduction of the independent variable), A (return to baseline), B (re-introduction of the independent variable).

Other behavioural studies use multiple independent variables varying the return to baseline. For example, the behavioural designs, ABCADA (Steele, 1967), ABCDA (Baird, 1969), and ABA (Johnson & Phillips, 1971) have appeared in music therapy and music education research literature (Furman, 1988; Madsen & Prickett, 1987).

An example of a complete reversal design with a group (as opposed to individual) experiment may be found in a study by Purvis (1971). In this study, three groups worked on arithmetic problems for five sessions. One group had rock-dance music as a background for working problems; another had rock-listening music as a background; and the third had no music. The design outline for the five sessions was as follows:

Group I   A   B   A   A   B
Group II   A   C   A   C   A
Group III   A   A   A   A   A

where A (i.e., baseline) = number of arithmetic problems worked

     B (i.e., the first independent variable) = rock-dance music as background

     C (i.e., the second independent variable) = rock-listening music as background

In this design two groups undergo a modified complete reversal pattern while a third group serves as a control. This is similar to a multiple-baseline design in that behaviour, measured but not treated within the multiple-baseline design, actually acts as a control condition to isolate the precise effect of the intervening independent

•

variable (Madsen & Yarbrough, 1975). It should be noted that the number of arithmetic problems worked is counted both during baseline (A) and during treatment (B and C), that is, measurement is continuous rather than discrete.

Sometimes it may be more useful to analyse the results of a study by charting the change in the dependent measures across time. To study the effects of behavioural self-assessment procedures on the acquisition of basic conducting techniques, Madsen and Yarbrough (1985) graphed the progress of the class as a whole across one term. Eight aspects of conducting technique were operationally defined (beat pattern, tempo, style, dynamics, eye contact, preparations, releases, and cueing), observation forms were developed for student use, and specific procedures for learning were developed. Students were videotaped conducting a pre-test in which they were told to demonstrate the eight aspects of conducting technique. They then conducted three videotaped practica during which they subsequently observed only preparations, beat patterns, eye contact, tempo, and releases; for the second practicum they observed an additional two categories, dynamics and cueing; for the third practicum, an additional category, style. Beginning with the fourth practicum, the music to be conducted was changed and the procedure just outlined was repeated. Thus the student was encouraged to build conducting technique through successive approximations and through behavioural self-assessment of progress. Following the sixth practicum, a post-test was recorded and evaluated to determine whether the student was able to transfer the skills learned to a new situation.

The following graph (see Figure 4) shows the percentages of correct responses for the pre- and post-tests and

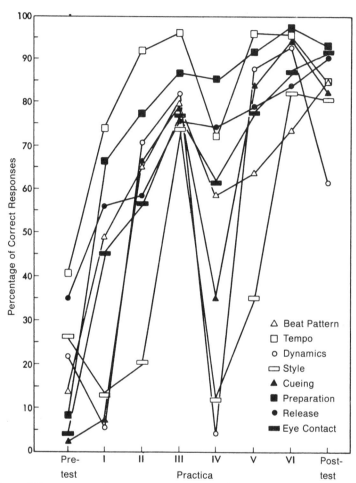

Figure 4 *Percentages of correct responses in conducting technique for pre-test, practica, and post-test.*

for each practicum. It demonstrates the effectiveness of the successive approximations approach with behavioural self-assessment. At the pre-test, students were achieving below 40% correct in every category of conducting technique. The graph clearly illustrates the categories assigned for initial practice and the result of above 40% correct for all five categories assigned. With the addition of two categories in the second practicum, students achieved above 50% correct in seven categories; and for the third practicum, above 70% correct in all eight categories. The graph shows that when the music was changed for the fourth practicum, students were able to transfer what they had learned for five of the categories, but were less successful for the remaining three. As they progressed through the fifth and sixth practica to the post-test, it is apparent that they were successful in achieving a high rate of accuracy in conducting technique (Madsen & Yarbrough, 1985, Chapter 5, pp. 96–123).

Summary

Systematic observation begins with thorough definition of observable, measurable behaviours. Observational techniques have been developed such that data can be collected during a session or afterwards using audio- or videotape. Both continuous and time-sampled protocols have been developed and are available.

In addition to observational collection of data, other descriptive techniques such as questionnaires and surveys remain viable alternatives for the illumination of current behaviour and opinions. However, these techniques, unlike systematic observation, are less useful in determining cause and effect relationships. Observation tools are reliable and valid dependent measures for use in behavioural or experimental designs. Practitioners will find them useful in recording and changing inappropriate as well as appropriate musical behaviours.

The primary practitioners of observational methodology are music educators and therapists. Researchers, teachers, and therapists from these groups are interested in techniques to effect change in learning and behaviour. Therefore, the systematic observation of behaviour becomes merely the first step in a continuing process of observe, record, treat, evaluate, observe, record, treat, evaluate, and so forth.

The technology and knowledge available to us today will enable those who choose research as their applied performing area to revolutionize the way we teach and learn music. Musicians have an opportunity now as never before to use technology to put innovation and creativity to work in expanding and revising the knowledge we now possess about music and musical behaviours. It is time for us to study how we form our musical ideas, how we communicate them, how we translate them into musical behaviours, and the effect of our musical behaviours upon listeners. Systematic observational methodology is an exciting avenue for gifted musician-scholars of the future.

References

Baird, S. (1969). A Technique to Assess the Preference for Intensity of Musical Stimuli in Young Hard-of-Hearing Children. *Journal of Music Therapy*, 6, 6–11.

Becker, W. C., Englemann, S. and Thomas, D. R. (1971). *Teaching: A Course in Applied Psychology*. Chicago: Science Research Associates.

Furman, C. E., ed. (1988). *Effectiveness of Music Therapy Procedures: Documentation of Research and Clinical Practice*. Washington, D. C.: National Association for Music Therapy.

Hall, R. V. and Van Houten, R. (1983). *Behavior Modification: The Measurement of Behavior*. Austin, TX: Pro-Ed.

Hauck, L. P. and Martin, P. L. (1970). Music as a Reinforcer in Patient-Controlled Time-Out. *Journal of Music Therapy*, 7, 43–53.

Johnson, J. M. and Phillips, L. L. (1971). Affecting the Behaviors of Retarded Children with Music. *Music Educators Journal*, 57, 45–46.

Jorgenson, H. (1971). Effect of Contingent Preferred Music in Reducing Two

Stereotyped Behaviors of a Profoundly Retarded Child. *Journal of Music Therapy*, 8, 139–145.

Jorgenson, H. and Parnell, M. K. (1970). Modifying Social Behaviors of Mentally Retarded Children in Music Activities. *Journal of Music Therapy*, 7, 83–87.

Madsen, Jr., C. H. and Madsen, C. K. (1981). *Teaching/Discipline: A Positive Approach for Educational Development*, 3rd Ed. Raleigh, NC: Contemporary Publishing Co.

Madsen, C. K. (1990). Measuring Musical Response. *Music Educators Journal*, 77, 26–28.

Madsen, C. K., Brittin, R. V. and Capperella-Sheldon, D. (1990). Empirical Measurement of the 'Aesthetic Response' to Music. Paper, presented at Research in Music Behavior Symposium, Cannon Beach, Oregon, March, 1991.

Madsen, C. K. and Prickett, C. A. (eds.) (1987). *Applications of Research in Music Behavior*. Tuscaloosa, AL: The University of Alabama Press.

Madsen, C. K. and Yarbrough, C. (1985). *Competency-Based Music Education*. Raleigh, NC: Contemporary Publishing Co.

Madsen, C. K. and Yarbrough, C. (1975). The Effect of Experimental Design on the Isolation of Dependent and Independent Variables. In C. K. Madsen, R. D. Greer and C. H. Madsen, Jr. (eds.), *Research in Music Behavior*. New York: Teachers College Press, 226–243.

Morgan, B. J. and Lindsley, O. R. (1966). Operant Preference for Stereophonic over Monophonic Music. *Journal of Music Therapy*, 3, 135–143.

O'Leary, K. D. and Becker, W. D. (1968–1969). The Effects of the Intensity of a Teacher's Reprimands on Children's Behavior. *Journal of School Psychology*, 7, 8–11.

O'Leary, K. D., Kaufman, K. F., Kass, R. E. and Drabman, D. S. (1970). The Effects of Loud and Soft Reprimands on the Behavior of Disruptive Students. *Exceptional Children*, 38, 145–155.

Performer 3.2. (1989). Cambridge, MA: Mark of the Unicorn.

Price, H. E. (1989). An Effective Way to Teach and Rehearse: Research Supports using Sequential Patterns. *Update: Applications of Research in Music Education*, 8, 42–46.

Purvis, J. (1971). The Effect of Rock Music on the Arithmetic Performance of Sixth-Grade Children. Unpublished master's thesis, Florida State University.

Rieber, M. (1969). The Effect of Music on the Activity Level of Children. *Psychonomic Science*, 3, 325–326.

Sharp, M. (1986). Relationships Among Model Performances and Performances by Piano Majors: Articulation and Dynamics in Selected Bach Fugal Excerpts. Unpublished doctoral dissertation, Louisiana State University.

Steele, A. L. (1967). Effects of Social Reinforcement on the Musical Preference of Mentally Retarded Children. *Journal of Music Therapy*, 4, 57–62.

Steele, A. L. (1971). Music Therapy: an Effective Solution to Problems in Related Disciplines. *Journal of Music Therapy*, 8, 131–139.

Wagner, M. J. (1975). Effect of Music and Biofeedback on Alpha Brainwave Rhythms and Attentiveness. *Journal of Research in Music Education*, 23, 3–13.

Yarbrough, C. (1975). Effect of Magnitude of Conductor Behavior on Students in Selected Mixed Choruses. *Journal of Research in Music Education*, 23, 134–138.

Yarbrough, C., Green, G., Benson, W. and Bowers, J. (1991). Inaccurate Singers: An Exploratory Study of Variables Affecting Pitch Matching. *Bulletin of the Council for Research in Music Education*, 107, 23–34.

Yarbrough, C. and Price, H. E. (1989). Sequential Patterns of Instruction in Music. *Journal of Research in Music Education*, 37, 179–187.

Yarbrough, C. and Price, H. E. (1981). Prediction of Performer Attentiveness Based on Rehearsal Activity and Teacher Behavior. *Journal of Research in Music Education*, 29, 209–217.

Yarbrough, C., Price, H. E. and Bowers, J. (1991). The Effect of Knowledge of Research on Rehearsal Skills and Teaching Values of Experienced Teachers. *Update: Applications of Research in Music Teaching*, 17–20.

Yarbrough, C., Speer, D. and Parker, S. (March 1990). Perception and Performance of Dynamics and Articulation Among Young Pianists. Paper presented at Music Educators National Conference, Washington, D. C.

6

Case Study and Action Research

CLEM ADELMAN AND ANTHONY E. KEMP

A case study is a detailed, 'rich' (Geertz, 1973) description of an aspect of a living or past culture within well delineated boundaries decided by the researcher. The intention is to provide details of events and their internal and external relationships with such accuracy and validity that all relationships between instances are made within the boundaries; and where they are not, adequate explanation of absence is provided. These criteria for case studies are very demanding and increase if the boundaries extend or the phenomena become more unpredictable or politicised. Thus case studies of change and innovation are often very difficult to fully accomplish in terms of the above criteria.

Case study was well defined as a methodology in the literature generated at the Chicago University School of Sociology back in the 1920s. By the 1950s the Harvard Business School had begun to define case study merely as a form of descriptive reporting, but since the 1970s case study has been revitalized as a methodical means of organizing and pursuing research data. The data is mainly qualitative, comprising observation both systematic and opportunistic, interview, questionnaire (but not survey) and documentary; quantitative data is incorporated where it also illuminates the case, making the relationships between instances more explanatory.

The researcher begins by collecting together all available information on the problem and makes notes of who to consult and where to look. If little has been recorded then the researcher has to begin to make observations, interview and so on. Whatever form the data takes at the outset there are likely to be gaps some of which are clearly apparent and can be filled by collecting new data; others become apparent and may have to wait upon the progress of the data collection before they can be pursued. The researcher should try to establish the meaning of each instance by collecting information from at least three sources. These sources may comprise different types of data but whatever form they take they should provide evidence to corroborate the meanings attributed to the phenomenon by the researcher. Discrepancies between accounts are pursued to fill the gaps. The pursuit of discrepancy may be a necessity at any time in the construction of the case but are most often realized during the writing of the study. At these points the researcher becomes acutely aware that the meaning or relationship of an instance cannot be stated with confidence. When attempting to use the methodology of case study for the first time the researcher would be well advised to decide on a narrowly bounded topic that provides ease of access to information sources. The case should not form part of any crucial evaluation or be set in a politicised context; such challenges may come subsequently. A useful way to begin would be to construct a case study of an aspect of the reader's own work. This encourages deep reflection on the significance, meaning and relationships of phenomena. Key moments in the story of the case are usually 'critical incidents', an unforeseen occurrence which reveals the latent positions or practices that the case is trying to describe.

Worthwhile books on the methodology and ethics of case study include Simons (1980) and Yin (1989). In this article we review three case studies in detail although we have to say at the outset that there is not a wide selection of case studies in the music education literature and even fewer attempts at action research. This is in part a reflection of the erstwhile dominance of experimental, psycho-statisical and survey methodologies in the study of music education.

Probably of even greater challenge to these methods is action research. This requires the researcher to move from the supposedly disinterested stance of the scientist to becoming engaged in the processes of designing and implementing, with the informed consent of participants, an intervention in their work or domestic practices. Since Kurt Lewin devised action research in the 1930s those that believe in a fully objective science of human practices have considered the inevitable confounding of variables and contamination of subjects to be without justification particularly for the procedure to incorporate the term 'research'. However this is, in part, a misunderstanding, as action research is an ethical, democratic procedure based on the willing and informed consent of participants in research into their own life and work. Action research is not in itself a methodology and may use a wide variety of methodologies, each in a valid way, to pursue the outcomes of the selected intervention. Lewin gave most significance to experimental designs to check on the efficacy of action research in the solution of complex social problems but also considered case study accounts very worthwhile but with less potential for generalization and replication. We found no examples of action research in music education although Maggie Teggin is shortly to incorporate action research in the new Postgraduate Certificate in Education music course at the School of Education, University of East Anglia.

Action research engages a willing group of implementors (teachers, musicians etc.) in sustained inquiry into problems that they come to realize they have in common. The groups have to be convened, methods of inquiry suggested, the process monitored and reports drafted. Lewin called the people who facilitated the process the 'change agent', so emphasizing the intended purpose of action research – to bring about desired change in working and domestic life through democratic participation in the actual process of change. Action research has a firm ethical base; coercive or individualistic social contexts are inimical to the process, yet such contexts may be the topic of inquiry.

Action research begins with the awareness by one or more people of a persistent 'problem', which seems to be an impediment to getting things done as well as they could be – there is an awareness of a gap between desirable and actual practice. Such conversations at work or in the wider community go on all the time and where they are crucial to people's quality of life they are usually carried forward as issues in local politics, union or other joint action to exert influence in order to change undesired circumstances. Action research may lead into and inform joint action of this sort. At its best, action research speaks of the reflective experiences of implementors of other's policy (including curriculum, assessment and pedagogy) and budget decisions.

The two, three or more who are aware of a persistent

problem meet to begin the discussions. They keep notes of their agreed and discrepant understandings of the problem addressing each of these separately if possible. After clarification, the group may make a decision to try a different way of working or organizing. They hold to this decision as a commitment for a fixed duration and keep individual records of the outcomes on their own patch. They report back to the group, and, together, discuss and make decisions, implement and monitor the developments. This is the procedure for action research. Now, at some point the group may seek advice on methods to research the problem and help with the analysis of what is becoming clearer but what may have wider implications. At this point they may call in a change agent. However, many examples of action research are projects where the change agent, having talked to many implementors, realizes a problem which is more widespread, seeks and gains funding and establishes further action research groups. The gap may be real or apparent and only research will clarify this, although it is the interpretation of the data by the action research group that counts as research. To positivists this seems like a dereliction of responsibility; too much reliance is placed on practitioners' accounts and interpretation. Lewin faced such objections from the scientific community. Careful, unhurried, reflexive participatory action research can help to make desirable changes in practice, in social relationships (including the pedagogical) and in attitude.

We sought within the literature of music education but failed to find action research studies that fulfilled all or most of the criteria of action research whether or not they were so called. In seeking research to cite in this chapter the criteria used were:

115

1. inquiry by a group, about issues of practice, using discussion, making group decisions about what to monitor.
2. keeping records of the inquiries,
3. meeting regularly to consider progress,
4. helping each other to reflect on the issues,
5. devising feasible ways of changing part of practice to effect desired change,
6. monitoring the consequences of the intervention and
7. evaluating individually and as a group the worth of the intervention and the status of the change, if any.

It is important that a cycle of action research is concluded by an evaluation of the endeavour in order to inform further cycles. One cycle takes about six months of part-time action research which is all that practitioners can usually allow. A change agent may be part of the research but is not essential. Group autonomy is the ideal. The wider uptake and influence of the action research on informing policy about curriculum, assessment, pedagogy and management should be noted and is, of course, desirable. Finally, issues for research may range from the innocuous to the highly contested, and clearly action research on the bland is a waste of human resources, although those holding budgets may sometimes wish to avoid controversial areas of practice. Action researchers should follow the wider interest through democratic participation which may include invitations to budget holders to participate.

We begin with case studies of music education. It is helpful to keep in mind the distinct constituents of case study as suggested by Stenhouse (1977): (a) the case record (notes, interviews, documents etc.), (b) the case history (how the case study proceeded) and (c) the case study itself. The 'York' project, first to be considered, has preserved a case record and part of a history but did not transform these into case studies.

Music in the Secondary School Curriculum

One of the most extensive case study type research projects in music education in the UK can be found in the archives of the Schools Council Project 'Music in the Secondary School Curriculum'. This five-year project was set up at the University of York in 1973 with John Paynter and a team of four. The project director's book (1982) in many ways admirably documents its outcomes, but for details of its structure and case history the reader must turn to the project's numerous news sheets, working papers, course papers and other materials. The project's intentions were to define more closely the place of music in the secondary school curriculum by:

1. developing new principles for school music that would take account of both interpretative and creative facets
2. widening the impact of the new principles through the production of guides and teaching materials
3. relating music to general considerations of the secondary school curriculum and organisation. (Schools Council, 1974a, p.52)

Paynter (1974) maintained from the outset that 'educational reform starts in the classroom' (p.1) and, through a process of meetings and conferences with teachers, headteachers, music advisers and other interested parties, developed a statement of guiding principles. This statement reveals the project team's central concern about the prevailing weakness of the secondary school music curriculum, which appeared at that time only to address the interests and aspirations of the most musically able pupils. A fundamentally new curriculum needed developing which would (a) be accessible to all pupils, (b) be seen as a part of a general policy for the arts in education, (c) offer pupils opportunities to develop imagination, sensitivity, inventiveness and delight, (d) be perceived as the main core of school music making, (e) to reveal the breadth of music's expressive possibilities, (f) allow pupils the opportunity of working with sound and thereby learning to control the medium, (g) embrace starting points which were not dependent upon any previous formal musical training, and (h) principally focus upon music making with the acquiescing of musical information existing merely as a support (Paynter, 1982, p. xiii).

Within the first year of the project, the team was encouraged by the extent of the response from Local Education Authorities. About 200 secondary schools were nominated to participate in the project and became linked through a national network of area organizations. These area groups operated as the focus for the work of pilot and trial schools (Schools Council, 1974b). Pilot schools undertook to work on the development of ideas and materials stimulated by an initial round of local conferences. Many of these pilot schools had programmes of experimental work already in progress and the project enabled their ideas to be developed, shared and, eventually tried by the wider group of trial schools. Curricular materials embodying the project's aims and philosophy were thus developed by pilot schools. These materials took the form of working units or modules which, together, it was hoped would cover all the conceivable facets of the music curriculum (ibid. p.3).

An afternoon conference was organized at York University for Chief Education Officers at which John Paynter outlined the project's aims. The meeting endorsed the view that area organizations were preferable to larger, regional ones and that the former would be well placed to co-ordinate the exploratory work being undertaken by the pilot schools as well as supervising the evaluation of materials in the trial schools.

By December 1975 a resource bank had been set up at the project's central office. This comprised all the project materials, working papers, topics and course papers as well as published resources considered to be in tune with the project's philosophy (Schools Council, 1975a). Lists of these materials were distributed together with listings of the 50 pilot schools and 67 trial schools (Schools Council, 1975b).

Freddie Sparrow (1975), Deputy Director of Studies at the Schools Council, writing in one of the project's news sheets, pointed out the fundamental importance of monitoring try-outs and collecting the essential basic data. Such data would take the form of

> Clear descriptions of the various modules and topics, together with accurate accounts of the contexts in which they are tried out and variations in outcomes. (Some of the data are 'hard' – size, sex, type, organisation of schools. The more intriguing data and perhaps the most vital are more subtle and much more difficult to obtain and present – 'atmosphere' of the school, background of the music teacher, attitudes to music of teacher and taught, authority structures, perception of role, local conditions affecting outcomes etc. What I think you have to do is to work on the basis of a number of 'Case Studies'. (p.5)

A number of changes in the membership of the project team may have prompted Paynter (1977a) to ensure continuity by reiterating the original aims of the project and identifying one or two gaps in its work. He was keen to ensure that sight was not lost of its original wide ranging intentions and produced a figure comprising 22 interlinked topics which mapped out the full extent of the project's domain. Paynter reported that work had started on the analysis of a large quantity of feedback from trial schools which he planned would be organized into a teachers' guide. What in fact emerged was the production of several *Working Papers* which were available on sale. These dealt with topics such as: 'The Influence of Pop on creative Music Making in the Classroom' (Piers Spencer); 'The Evaluation of Classroom Music Activities' (John Paynter); 'The Organisation of Small-Group Work in the Classroom' (Joan Arnold). These were not case studies, although with their detailed knowledge the team probably had the data with which to undertake and probably complete case studies.

Many of the teachers associated with the project took part in an exercise in May 1976 in which they were invited to send their views as to what constituted 'good classroom practice' in music (Paynter, 1977b). Within the same *Working Paper* Paynter summarised the responses and, appended an Evaluation Checklist for teachers. This was assembled under six headings: (a) Objectives, General Philosophy of Music in Education – the School's Policy for Music, (b) Classroom Organisation, Preparation and Planning, (c) Lesson Content; Progress of the Work; Pupils' Development, (d) Discipline and Pupil/Teacher Relationships, (e) General Considerations: Organisation, Planning, Materials and Equipment, (f) Teaching Techniques. The Checklist, rather curiously, was organised in two separate sections, the first headed 'General Class Music Activities', covering areas (a) to (d), and the second 'The Evaluation of Creative Music-Making' comprised (e) and (f).

The following list shows a few selected items from the Checklist:

(a)   Are the pupils directly involved with music as *sound*? (or if not does the material prepared quickly lead towards such an involvement?).

Are the activities likely to develop aural awareness and discrimination? Are the pupils using their ears?

Are there opportunities for pupils to take decisions? Opportunities to 'interpret' information and ideas?

Is the material/activity likely to enable pupils to extend their range of musical experience *by their own initiative?*

Is the material/activity essentially musical?

(b)   Is there *evidence* that the teacher has prepared the material/ activities carefully?

Does the teacher keep careful records of work? Is there an overall scheme of work? Does the scheme allow for unexpected developments?

Is the work planned applicable to all pupils in the class whatever their musical background?

Is the teacher secure in what he/she has planned?

(c)   Is the teacher able to involve everyone?

Is the teacher able to convey to the pupils the relevance and importance of what they are doing?

Is the teacher enthusiastic? And is the enthusiasm communicated?

Does the teacher display musical sensitivity and imagination?

Does the teacher *teach?* (i.e. does he, by his actions, planning etc. fulfill his role as a *educator?*

(d)   Is the teacher able to exercise control through interest and involvement of the class? Are the pupils on his wave-length?

Is the teacher giving sufficient guidance without over-direction?

121

(e)   Does the teacher's planning/scheme of work make possible the exploration of a variety of styles of music, both new and old? Does the planning/method of work make it possible to develop a variety of musical skills and techniques (including the so-called 'traditional' skills) from the basis of creative activities? If the strategy involves work in small groups have the optimum group sizes been determined?

(f)   Is the teacher personally convinced about what he/she and the class are doing?

Is there sufficient discussion of the topic(s) between teacher and class prior to division into small groups?

Is there evidence of genuine exploration and discovery in pupils' activities?

Does the teacher make worthwhile links between pupils' music and appropriate examples of existing music?

Is there adequate opportunity for pupils to perform their music? Do the pupils appear to derive satisfaction from performing their music?

Is there care in performance? Is there evidence of aural sensitivity?

(Paynter, 1977c, pp.2–6).

Clearly these are questions which could have been specifically pursued through case studies.

In one of the last *News Sheets* a Head of Music wrote

The girls in this Grammar School are taught traditional skills in reading and playing music. There are examinations to be prepared for, and concerts to be produced, and it is not possible therefore to allocate much time to creative work at present. However, when we have a comprehensive intake in a few years' time, I am sure that creative music will play a much larger part in the curriculum. (Schools Council, 1979, p.4)

One wonders how this teacher, whose attitudes had already begun to show modest signs of shifting, fared in the years which were to follow. Swanwick's (1979) model for the structure of the music curriculum soon was to endorse the project's belief in the centrality of composition and performance in classroom music, and to become a feature of the 'new orthodoxy'. Case studies carried out over the duration of the whole project could have provided some important evidence about teachers' developing attitudes, their relationships with the project, and an understanding of how such divergencies came about.

In summing up the project, Paynter (1982) regretted the fact that the term 'creative music' had taken on such an exclusive meaning, being used by teachers in some quarters to express their unease about the project. There was also a tendency amongst some to adopt the term as encapsulating all aspects of the music curriculum which were experimental or untried. He thought that the time had come to stop talking about 'creative music', maintaining that 'all knowledge and skill can be put to creative use' (p.137).

Paynter's final remarks do not detract from the project's achievements. The dissemination centres had by that time been operating for nearly four years and were being largely successful in preparing teachers for the eventual arrival of the new General Certificate of Secondary Education Examination for sixteen year-old pupils, in which composition, performing and listening were stated as the three equal components of the music curriculum. It could be maintained that it was due to the pioneering work of the project, that a significant number of secondary school music teachers were ready for this initiative and, indeed, in many instances were active in pressing for these changes. The work of the project could be said to have come to an end when the ground-swell of this new thinking, encapsulated in the slogan 'music for all', caught the remaining teachers up in a flurry of project-type courses and conferences.

The second piece of research described here provides examples of case studies which attempt to change classroom teaching through action research. Although time and other pressures precluded the completion of the full cycle of action research the project demonstrated that teachers are able to conduct evaluative research into their own work and report this in case study detail. Clearly the detail is more extensive than can be reported here.

Classroom Issues in Assessment and Evaluation in the Arts

This piece of work, in contrast to the previous project, had a more manageable brief and operated over a shorter period of time. As its title implies, it spanned all the arts and comprised eleven topics involving art, dance, drama and poetry as well as music, these ranging in focus from age three to nineteen. The project was set up by Berkshire Local Education Authority in 1986 with support from the Schools Curriculum Development Committee's 'Arts in Schools Project' and was guided by Veronica Treacher. Clem Adelman was the research consultant to the project.

In describing the work Hamish Preston, the LEA adviser with responsibility for the conduct of the project, described how the teachers in the team each identified a set of personal concerns related to the process of assessment in the arts where they felt that they would benefit from a more thorough examination of their own practice than was normally possible. The principal questions, pursued by the team, were

> How do you encourage children to work from their own inner experience and by what criteria do you recognise such authen-

ticity? Is it possible, or indeed desirable to eradicate the element of personal judgement when assessing pupils' work? What manifest themselves in the end product? How can you take account of the qualities like awareness, responsiveness and resourcefulness in recording pupils' progress? How can the teacher encourage children to develop their own powers of discrimination? (Berkshire Education Authority, 1989, p.7)

Preston goes on to describe how he saw 'the procedures of action research move practical questions into the theoretical area which, according to cherished myth, is of little relevance to a working teacher' (p.7). The team, he said, were able to provide examples of moments when what was happening, *while* it was happening, crystalised a doubt or aspiration, 'giving it form and therefore making it capable of intellectual confrontation and development. Ideas and theories about curriculum became tangible and dynamic' (ibid, pp. 7 & 8). Two of the eleven case studies focused specifically upon the assessment of music listening: 'Assessing listening skills in music (10–11 years)', undertaken by Pamela Hibbert, and 'Encouraging and assessing listening skills in music (13–14 years)' by David Soby.

Hibbert set out to collect classroom evidence of children's listening responses to particular tasks. Over a period of two terms she monitored a class of top juniors by tape-recording the lessons and discussions with the children, keeping her own observational notes as well as those from an independent observer. Her prepared sequences of lessons fell into three main types in which different ways of listening were emphasized: (a) listening to music where no physical response was required, (b) listening activities involving answering questions verbally or writing answers to a listening exercise, and (c) group composi-

125

tions. The project report documents a selection of four separate lessons, each followed by a description of events, an evaluation and discussion to which Hibbert and her observer had contributed.

In her conclusions Hibbert was able to demonstrate the degree to which her interpretations of her data helped her to develop her thinking and inform her future classroom work in music listening. She had learned that:

> 1. It is not necessary or possible or desirable to include every element of musical activity as separate entities in every lesson... concentration on one or two...seems more effective.
> 2. Learning by aural means seems to aid concentration (listening) and memory, especially where it is accompanied by creative musical activity.
> 3. In composing activities, the children were assessing themselves. Because they had all participated they felt qualified to comment upon the others.
> 4. The creative lessons...were by far the most successful in terms of listening, and learning....Getting children to be creative first and then introducing them to the compositions of others seems...a better way of addressing the common complaint that children don't listen.
> 5. Conventional listening, of the apparently non-active and non-visibly engaged kind is impossible to assess but of central importance.
> 6. By observing the way the children behaved and listening to them during the composing process, it was possible to assess their grasp of musical concepts derived from listening....An experienced teacher's judgement via observation carried out during practical music-making sessions, is a valid method of assessing.
> 7. This case study revealed in terms of my own practice that an approach through composition was the most rewarding and relevant to pursue as a means of improving listening skills. (ibid., p.53)

Soby's case study, in contrast, focused on middle secondary pupils and attempted to address the problem concerning a discrepancy between the aspirations embodied in his aims and his actual practice. He had, for many years, been concerned about the apparent inability of many of his pupils to listen carefully and with concentration – or even to remain silent for any length of time. He began to question some of his criteria which he had considered essential to good listening: was silence necessary? Were there different ways of listening? Did today's pupils have different listening skills? How did we assess how well pupils were listening? Was their listening capacity improved when they were performing or composing their own music? How did pupils listen to music at home?

Soby monitored eight lessons with a class of twenty-five 13–14 year-olds to whom he administered a questionnaire and subsequently recorded whole class and group activities and discussions. More than half the class were interviewed on a number of occasions, and an observer attended half the sessions. Three types of lesson were prepared: the first concentrated on learning and rehearsal leading to performance; the second on composition for performance; and the third consisted of a single lesson of listening to two extracts that the pupils had neither played or composed. All the activities were designed to encourage good listening and the lessons, it was hoped, would provide an exact definition of his and the pupils' assessment criteria and procedures.

The principal outcome of this research for Soby was the realization that the pupils' listening habits were substantially different from his own and that he tended to impose his own personal listening standards on to them. On questioning his pupils about their patterns of music listening at home he learned that it predominantly consisted of background music which accompanied other activities. There was little evidence of pupils listening to music for its own sake, tending to explain why there was an inability to keep quiet and concentrate solely on a piece of music in the classroom.

However, Soby considered that listening was central to music in the classroom, embodied within the aspects of performance and composition. If this was the case, then what form should listening take? The outcome of his research tended to suggest to him 'that the quality of their listening can be more accurately judged by observing the process of problem-solving, choosing and organising' (p. 193). Rather than insisting on his own form of 'rapt' silence, it would be more appropriate to allow the pupils to work against a noisy background, a situation in which they appeared to be entirely able to operate. Furthermore, it became obvious to him that the pupils became self-conscious about the demands of the pure listening type of lesson. Listening was better approached, he discovered, through the more active modes of creating music. 'The pupils most enjoyed working together, solving problems together, experimenting, exercising their powers of discrimination and judgement'. (p. 194) The quality of listening skills, he believed, could be more appropriately assessed through the depth of perception of the pupils' own evaluation of these activities.

This research gave the teachers much greater support in defining the research agenda and in the interpretation of the data than the previous project. In the Berkshire project the teachers, having identified their issues, researched these with guidance on method and, eventually, on presentation from Veronica Treacher.

The third piece of research comprises case studies constructed by professional researchers in which considerable effort was made into representing the voices of teachers, pupils, parents and administrators. Some generalizations, arrived at through comparison amongst the case studies, are made in this research. Stake, one of the research team, had, back in the 1960s, been instrumental in reviving interest in the use of case studies. Earlier he had developed psycho-statistical methods and applied them to evaluation. Indeed, he, together with Cronbach, Campbell and Glass, had helped define the use and limitations of quasi-experiment in social research, and subsequently advocated the validity of naturalistic methodologies such as case study. Music education research, in common with most evaluation and social research, has tended to overlook or ignore the subsequent critical developments by many of those who made the original major advances in the methodologies.of the psycho-statistical and the quasi-experimental.

Custom and Cherishing: The Arts in Elementary Schools

These eight case studies of arts teaching in elementary school classrooms in the USA were completed over a three-year period (Stake, Bresler & Mabry, 1991). The project concerned itself less with the question of what the children were learning but more about the opportunities being offered for learning. The project team set out to study ordinary classrooms believing these often to be under-studied in favour of educational critiques of good and bad teaching. The outcome of this all too frequently, they believed, was that studies all too frequently fail to portray ingenious and tenacious efforts of ordinary teachers.

Although starting out with a complex matrix-type research scheme, the team soon became more narrowly focused onto six main issues: identifying whether or not (a) attention was being given to aesthetics, beauty and understanding in the arts, (b) arts activities were being integrated into other subjects due to limited time and, if so, the effect that this had on arts education goals, (c) teaching materials were being expanded beyond European culture towards popular and multicultural arts, (d) curricular and organizational expectations pressurised teachers into being more authoritative in the classroom resulting in less attention being given to arts events outside, (e) advocates of a more discipline-based or high quality arts curricula were to be found in elementary schools, and (f) forms of arts education leadership were to be found (Stake, Bresler & Mabry, 1992, p. 9).

In a very illuminating way, and particularly helpful for the purposes of this chapter, Stake et al describe their approach to case study research in some detail; wishing to preserve and document what the observer sees and to interpret these observations as holding meanings which may not be immediately apparent to others. The relevance of dialogue and contextual detail are emphasized not only to portray the event but to develop 'issue-based assertions' (p. 11). The research approach was described as being:

1. *Naturalistic* – the team preferred not to use questionnaires, because they felt that these tended to direct attention away from everyday pursuits. They maintained that 'happenings are best understood with a careful attention to their contexts'.

2. *Service-orientated* – the research should serve those most closely involved in arts teaching and policy-making. The research should be useful for different types of people and therefore its usefulness and potential in this respect needed regular checking.

3. *Empathic* – because the research 'attends to the intentions of the people studied, their value commitments, their frames of reference'. Although the team started with their own notions of what was important, increasingly they tried to highlight those issues of importance to those closely associated with the case studies (p. 11).

Thus the researchers tried to emphasize the uniqueness of the situation as much as the general.

> Every site has its own story to tell and none is adequately representative of others. Still in each, most readers see parallels reflecting and informing about their own arts classrooms. A special aspect of the particularisation in this report is our rather personalistic presentation. Many educational researchers consider staff and student personalities facades which must be penetrated. We consider personalities to be determining factors, thus a central part of the stories. For all the effort to cast education into a technical and standardized operation, it remains greatly a product of spontaneity and intuition on both sides of the desk. The particulars of arts education cannot be understood, we believe, without the personalistic dimensions. (p. 12)

Space does not permit a description and discussion of the eight projects. What perhaps is more important for the reader is to gather some understanding of the nature of the case studies and what they reveal about music (and arts) education in the late twentieth century in one of the wealthiest nations of the world. However, it must be appreciated that, in doing this, the greater part of the report in which the nature and contexts of the schools, the topics of the case studies, descriptions of classroom encounters, transcripts of interviews and discussions, and their conclusions are omitted. Also omitted, therefore, are the details in which are embedded the quality and intensity of the inquiry and its deeper search for the teachers' constructs. The reader is therefore particularly encouraged to pursue this material as exemplars of research methodology of this kind.

The main conclusions arrived at from a composite view of the eight case studies relate to

1. *The Marginality of Arts in the Schools:* The research team reported that commonly music was taught for about 30 minutes per week, 'normally' taught by a specialist. The researchers emphasized that there was no typical child, no typical school and no typical arts education in America. Out of school provision was even more uneven and dependent upon the particular interests and abilities of teachers. The rather depressing message from the community to the school was

> Keep art and music a part of the curriculum; keep it modest and conventional; continue the traditional performances and exhibits....Teaching the arts for their cultural substance and their centrality to human expression was to be found schoolwide in perhaps a third of our schools, in only one or two classrooms in a second third of our schools, and essentially not at all in the remaining third'. (p. 342)

2. *Instructional Reform:* Within the case studies the team did not study forthcoming decisions, implementation of choice, and the generality of problems and therefore were

not in a position to recommend courses of action needing to be taken. Instead, five strategies were commented upon which, it was thought, might lead to improvement. These were : (a) A curriculum improvement strategy, reforming what teachers teach and changing the notion of what schools can best contribute to children's education.

> But as to specific facts, skills and attitudes, it is not apparent that different teachers should all be teaching the same things. Teacher responsibility for what they teach is important. Accountability can be achieved by encouraging the individual teacher to work from a syllabus if that brings out their best teaching but, if it does not, to advance alternative conceptualization's and activities. Often at the expense of standardization, it should be important to teachers to foster uniqueness in personal perception, their own as well as their students. (p.343)

(b) The need to integrate the arts with personal cherishing, perhaps by persuading teachers to commit themselves to a 'small number of arts learnings', particularly if these relate to ideas that the teacher holds dear. 'Moving from the teacher's personal cherishing to the essences of the arts is no small task...but the strategy seems worth further consideration' (p. 343). (c) Paying attention to artistic activity in the community and developing the notion that 'most of the arts of the home, shopping mall, park, concert hall, church, and stadium are educating, some commendably...arts education is vitalized by signs that people care' (p. 344). (d) Changing the underlying attitudes of teachers and administrators, particularly the latter who saw the arts more as a promotional device for the schools than as an education in its own right. Staff development programmes appeared to be failing, allowing the arts to remain in a marginalized role.

3. *The Authorities:* The researchers were particularly concerned that there appeared to be a gulf between teachers and those who speak and write about music and art education. Although some teachers and school authorities occasionally referred to the work of advocates of high quality art in general education they still nevertheless gave them low priority in their teaching. On the other hand the team also felt that the authorities were out of touch with the practitioners and there appeared to be no alliance between them. One problem, it was felt, 'was that the leaders were calling for revolutionary change whereas the teachers held little hope even for evolutionary change and considered protectionist strategies more appropriate than expansionist' (p. 345).

We have reviewed these three studies in some detail partly because they are not widely known and partly because they are some of the few examples of published case studies in music education. The British Journal of Music Education, which over the years has included a number of case study type reports, has recently published a piece by Davies (1992) which is worthy of particular note. The theoretical and empirical boundaries of this study of children's song compositions are explicitly identified by Davies. The research took place in school classrooms during regular lessons and songs were collected from 32 children aged five to seven over a period of 18 months. Davies provides transcriptions of part or all of 29 songs and a descriptive analysis of each. Relationships between the instances are made through comparisons on criteria drawn from the data collected. Davies concludes

> The sequential model of development needs to be complemented by detailed consideration of individual children. The

broad general overview provides valuable reference points; but in the arts it is particularly important to recognise and to celebrate the individual's personal exploration and statement as well as to know in what way people are the same. (p. 47)

Without mentioning the kind of methodology adopted, Davies presents a strong and convincing argument for the adoption of the case study approach in this kind of inquiry.

Conclusion

We were unable to find accounts of work in the field which met the criteria of action research but, hopefully, others will continue and build upon the kind of achievements reported in the Berkshire project. Case studies can provide detailed, authentic accounts of a phenomenon in context, avoiding the fragmentation of the experimental, the generalities of the survey and the descriptive limitations of statistics. In case study the reader is able to trace the process of curriculum development and the implementation of pedagogy and assessment. This helps in an effective way to support informed development in education. Action research tests the feasibility of plans and of policy at the point of implementation. Obviously, case study and action research make visible the details of practice, and thus, make for a vulnerability to direct criticism that can be avoided in the three other methodologies. However, if honest public discussion and argument is to take place, then the issues have to be accessible and this includes the instances and contexts of case study at the very least.

We have given a summary of the methodology of case study and provided illustrative extracts from an influential and incipient project, of studies written by teachers about their own work and by professional educational researchers about teaching in school systems. We hope very much that the reader will take the initiative to pursue the methodology of case study and adopt the procedures of action research.

References

Berkshire Local Education Authority (1989). *Classroom Issues in Assessment and Evaluation in the Arts*. Reading: Berkshire Local Education Authority.

Davies, C. (1992). Listen to My Song: A Study of Songs Invented by Children Aged 5 to 7 Years. *British Journal of Music Education*, 9, 19–48.

Geertz, C. (1973). Thick Description: Toward an Interpretative Theory of Culture. In C Geertz (ed.) *The Interpretation of Cultures: Selected Essays by Clifford Geertz*. New York: Basic Books.

Paynter, J. (1974). Music in the Secondary School Curriculum. *News Sheet*, 1, 1.

Paynter, J. (1977a). Keeping Objectives in View. *News Sheet*, 7, 1–3.

Paynter, J. (1977b). The Evaluation of Classroom Music Activities: Music in the School Curriculum. *Working Paper 4*, Part 1. York: University of York.

Paynter, J. (1977c). The Evaluation of Classroom Music Activities: Evaluation Checklists. *Working Paper 4*, Part 2. York: University of York.

Paynter, J. (1982). *Music in the Secondary School Curriculum*. Cambridge: Cambridge University Press.

Schools Council (1968). *Enquiry 1: Young School Leavers*. London: HMSO.

Schools Council (1974a). *Project Profiles*. London: Schools Council.

Schools Council (1974b). 200 Schools: Regional Organisation. *News Sheet*, 2, 1.

Schools Council (1975a). Editorial. *News Sheet*, 5, 1.

Schools Council (1975b). Resources Bank – Contents. *News sheet*, 5 (Supplement).

Schools Council (1979). No Comment. *News Sheet*, 10, 4.

Simons, H. (ed.) (1980). Towards a Science of the Singular. *CARE Occasional Publications No. 10*. Centre for Applied Research in Education, University of East Anglia.

Sparrow, F. (1975). Some Thoughts on Evaluation. *News Sheet*, 5, 5–7.

Stake, R., Bresler, L. and Mabry, L. (1991). *Custom and Cherishing: The Arts in Elementary Schools*. Urbana, IL.: Council for Research in Music Education/University of Illinois.

Stenhouse, L. (1977). Exemplary Case Studies: Towards a Descriptive Educational Research Tradition Grounded in Evidence: a proposal for submission to the SSRC.

Swanwick, K. (1979). *A Basis for Music Education*. Slough: NFER.

Yin, R. K. (1989). Case Study Research: Design and Methods. *Applied Social Research Methods Series, Vol. 5*. London and New Delhi: Sage Publications.

Writing Research Reports

ANTHONY E. KEMP

Before embarking upon report writing it is important that writers should consider very carefully the likely readership because this may influence the content and style of writing in a number of ways. For example, the style of presentation adopted will vary according to whether groups of researchers, teachers, administrators or government officials are being addressed. Different groups will not only require varying levels of explanation, but the methods adopted for presenting the results as well as the foci for their discussion and interpretation may also differ.

Research reports tend to follow a common structure whether they take the form of a thesis for the award of a research degree, a conference or seminar paper, or a journal article. One often finds that people engage in a natural progression from one form of writing to another. A discussion paper written, say, for a small group of colleagues may, later, become expanded and be re-worked for delivery at a conference, subsequently to be published in the conference proceedings or as a journal article.

This chapter will largely concentrate on the preparation of these kinds of report where the length will be restricted by the timetable structure of the conference or seminar in question or the constraints of the journal that has been selected. Conferences normally publish calls for papers and most journals print guidelines for contributors; persons preparing submissions for either are strongly advised to heed these in every detail. Those whose responsibility it is to select papers for conference programmes or who review articles for journals will know that all too frequently papers are received from authors who have tended to disregard the very guidelines which have been principally formulated to assist and encourage them.

The golden rule for anyone preparing to write a research report is to ensure that the reader is provided with all the necessary information to repeat the research design, using the same procedures for collecting data and analysing them. These shorter forms of research reporting where space is usually limited, perhaps to two or three thousand words, require the writer to be particularly disciplined, firstly about omitting material which does not relate directly to a description of the research in question and secondly guarding against the tendency to waste words and to write in an unnecessarily expansive style. Writing a good research report is a time-consuming task and it is likely that it will go through a number of drafts until all blemishes are removed and the language adopted clear, direct and informative. If a word processor is available for use this is an invaluable aid in moving from one draft to the next without the necessity of re-typing or cutting and pasting. As this form of technology becomes within the means of more people, those contemplating programmes of writing should seriously consider purchasing a computer which will handle both word processing and data storage.

The structure advocated in this chapter is generally accepted as fairly standard procedure for research writing for most methodologies. However it must be noted that there are some marked differences between some research approaches and others, and these will be mentioned in passing. For example historical, and to a large extent comparative research, do not always adopt the kind of structure referred to here, or at least, not in the same kind of way that experimental or observational research does.

Historical and comparative research may move through the same kind of phases: identifying a problem or a question, collecting the evidence, interpreting the evidence, and, finally, reaching conclusions. Although the research process itself may have adopted this progression, the actual research report may take the form of a more continuous prose with the text organized under subheadings which relate to different aspects of the research problem. The reader, more interested in historical or comparative research, who may feel that this chapter has unduly concentrated on other styles of research reporting in music education is encouraged to consult, particularly the historical work of Rainbow (1967, 1970, 1991); Cox (1990, 1992); Koza (1990); and Southcott (1990); and the comparative accounts of Lepherd (1985, 1986, 1988); Bartle (1986, 1988); Paynter (1987); and Okafor (1991). Even in those cases where the structure described here is adopted, it may not be used as explicitly as it is by experimental researchers. For various examples of research reports which generally 'unfold' in this way, but without adhering rigidly to the structure suggested here, see Kwami (1991); Swanwick (1991); Verney (1991); and Davies (1992). Helpful examples of short, condensed seminar-type papers have been written by Crowther, Durkin, Shire and Hargreaves (1985); Fiske (1985); Kemp (1985); Welch (1985); and Hassler (1989).

Statement of the Problem

By the time the reader has completed the research and is ready to 'write up', the nature of the problem will be very familiar. During the research many people may have enquired about it, and therefore it should be fairly easy to state simply, clearly and precisely the particular aspects of the problem that have been pursued. This section is essentially an introduction and sets out to explain to the reader what the aims were and the reasons why the research was necessary in the first place. It should also serve the purpose of catching the interest of the reader or the conference participant through a clear communication of the writer's enthusiasm and grasp of the topic.

Review of Related Literature

By the time the reporting stage arrives, a very good grasp and knowledge of a large body of literature relating to the research will have been gained. There will be very little space for this to be described in detail and considerable discipline should be exercised to ensure that only that material which relates directly to the research will be recorded. The organization of this section is very critical and it is often helpful to group the references together around a major point which needs making before proceeding to the next in the same way. Refer to pieces of research with the use of the author's family name only, followed by the date in parentheses. Here are examples of two different ways of doing this:

> Improved channels of communication between researchers and teachers have been called for at various times (Brand, 1984; Kemp, 1987; Scott, 1990).

141

Swanwick and Tillman (1986) analysed children's compositions and constructed a model describing a sequence of development.

The approach to reviewing the literature must be both analytical and critical. In analysing research reports the reader is required to develop a full understanding of the underlying rationale, procedural detail, methods of analysing the evidence, dimensions of the arguments and logic of the conclusions. Once this level of understanding has been achieved, the reader will be in a stronger position to evaluate the research, identifying its strengths and weaknesses, and appraising it within the context of other literature in the field.

In journal articles and conference papers, where space is limited, the review will be restricted to a discussion of those studies which lie closest to the current research: those which have helped in developing the research area and hypotheses, and those which have influenced the research design and procedures. There will not be space to refer to all the research which might have been included in a longer thesis. Having narrowed down the material, analyse each piece to locate the most salient points and assemble these by clustering together those which relate to one another. Frequently, it will be found that authors commence a review by making the more general points first, referring to the research which relates to the problem generally. Having done this they may then deal with the more specific aspects of the problem as represented by the clusters of observations that have already been assembled. An important part of the review may involve highlighting a disagreement between two studies or between two groups of researchers; it will be important to discuss this, particularly if the current research has set out to clarify this issue. Alternatively, it may be felt that a piece of research, whilst relating closely to that being undertaken, has some in-built weaknesses or has misinterpreted the results; in this case the criticism will be approached objectively and fairly, and perhaps showing how the current work has learned from it.

Absolute accuracy over reporting the research of others is imperative. Throughout the process of writing reviews, authors have to be very clear in their minds concerning the distinction between what has been read in research reports written by others and what are their own comments, analyses and criticism of them. Whether a brief quotation of a significant and critical passage is supplied or a paraphrase of what has been written by another author is made, it is of paramount importance that the reference is cited. Failing to do so will imply that the writer him or herself is the author of the passage and this constitutes a very serious academic misdemeanour, namely, plagiarism.

Writing a review of the literature takes skill, and, as indicated above, its preparation will move through a number of drafts before satisfaction is achieved. Economy of words must be an important criterion and, where a common observation can be made which relates to several studies, the technique identified in the first example of referencing shown above can be adopted. By the end of the review it should be clear to the reader exactly how the research question has evolved – through a thorough search and examination of the literature and the precise way in which it emerges from it. Good examples of research reports which display clarity of purpose and review relevant research economically and analytically are to be found in Taebel (1990); Sloboda and Howe (1991); Standley and Madsen (1991); and Bergee (1992).

It may be helpful to recall the extent that the reader was dependent upon accurate and analytical reviews when the literature search was being undertaken. Make every attempt to be as supportive as possible to those researchers who are to follow.

Description of the Research Design and Measurement Techniques.

In more experimentally orientated research the description of the design and the measurement techniques may be dealt with under their separate headings. Clearly the more descriptive research methodologies will not involve formal measurement techniques although it is possible that observational techniques and questionnaires will require description in some detail at this point.

In circumstances where groups of samples were tested full details of the sampling techniques should be supplied; if a multi-group strategy is adopted, with or without a control group, it is important to describe how possible intervening factors such as age or gender have been dealt with, perhaps by matching or by using some form of covariate analysis. In instances where classes or individual students were studied as the focus for case studies or action research, it is important to supply the reader with a brief but all-embracing description of all the likely background factors such as age, sex and social background which may have a bearing on the research outcomes. Where educational institutions were the focus, the social and economic climate, their educational ethos, curricular and organizational features may require careful reporting.

The next step is to report the methods which were used to collect the data. This may have been through postal questionnaire, group or individual testing sessions, observation or through participant observation. In cases where other researchers were employed it is important for the reader to know what measures were taken to eliminate inter-researcher/observer variation. If scripted instructions were given to research assistants these should be supplied in the text. If inter-judge or observer variance was tested for statistically these procedures should be briefly documented.

Where a published test was used it is important for the details of this to be supplied along with a note about the test's published reliability rating. Include also details of the particular edition of the test and its reference (author's name and date of publication). If a test instrument was specifically devised for the research, it may be possible, depending on its length, to include this in an appendix. However, it might be appropriate to include a sample item or two in the body of the script to give the reader an accurate idea about the nature of the instrument. Where a test was devised, brief details of any item analysis or trialling that was carried out should be reported. Also, consider providing the reader with an address from where a copy of the full test may be obtained.

The final part of this section will deal with any statistical procedures used to analyse the data or to test for significant differences. If standard procedures were used these will not require description and may be merely reported along with the results in the next section. Neither raw scores nor details of calculations need reporting; only those procedures, if not standard, should be described. Wherever possible supply as much information as possible in tabular form. Carefully constructed tables save considerable amounts of text and are far easier for the reader to comprehend. Study Nagel, Himle and Papsdorf (1989) for a good example of a clear description of a research design in which the composition of experimental and control groups are outlined together with the research procedures and test instruments.

Statement of Results

This section and the one that follows may be combined in the more descriptive or qualitative research methodologies. In experimental research, however, it is often helpful for the reader to supply a statement of the results which is as brief as possible and which is accompanied by relevant tables, diagrams or graphs. It is important not to get involved in any discussion or interpretation of the results at this point; merely state the outcomes of the analyses as described earlier. Where a number of hypotheses were tested the results should be given in the same order as the hypotheses were originally described (and adopting the same numbering). For a helpful example of a fairly complex statement of results which includes tables and figures see Hassler, Birbaumer and Feil (1987).

Discussion and Interpretation of the Results

In this section the statement of the results are returned to in an attempt to analyse and interpret them and to make educational sense of them. This will be carried out within the context of the research reviewed earlier, making observations about the results in relation to earlier studies. The results should be discussed from a number of different perspectives to clarify the ways in which they relate to the body of research and contribute to it. At this stage it may be appropriate to report further analyses carried out which were not initially planned. This sometimes becomes necessary simply because the emerging results provide unexpected outcomes which may require further enlightenment. Where further analyses have been carried out, these may require additional tables or figures to present the results as clearly as possible. Sometimes the results reveal that a mistake occurred in, say, sampling, or at the testing stage, or that with hindsight an inappropriate test was used; in such instances the researcher is advised to include an admission of the weakness in the discussion and any temptation to conceal the mistake should be resisted. To concede shortcomings in research design or administration is the hallmark of a researcher who is both meticulous and fully aware of research discipline.

Conclusions

This final section serves as a summary in which the author may draw together all the important threads of the research in a statement about the main outcomes. It provides an opportunity to state clearly what the research has achieved, to evaluate it and to assess its significance. Great care should be taken not to overstate the degree of importance of the results; where they are modest, concede the fact. Where results have emerged as not significant (say, $p = .06$) that is the end of the matter. Remember

147

that results are either significant or not significant; they cannot be 'nearly significant'. Be cautious about claiming generalizability; the results relate to the samples tested and may not generalize to other samples and populations. Sloboda and Howe (1991) and Hassler, Birbaumer and Feil (1987) have provided excellent examples of discussions and conclusions which display this kind of caution concerning the general application of results.

The researcher may find him or herself in the position to make recommendations about future educational practice or provision. In addition, some researchers make a point of discussing their ideas for future research and share such hypotheses which have arisen directly out of their results. This assists the reader undertaking a literature search to identify a research topic to place the research into context, particularly in connection with future developments in the field.

References and Bibliography

Generally, research papers and articles require a list of references rather than a bibliography. The essential difference between the two is that references comprise works which have been cited within the text; bibliography, on the other hand, are works which the author has read for background information and which are being recommended to the reader.

The method of listing these tends to be similar although there are some slight variations of use within different journals. The method adopted in this book, except for the chapter on historical research, sometimes known as the 'Harvard' method, is that frequently associated with the social sciences. The following examples

148

show the kind of format which may be adopted for listing different types of publication:

A book:
> Bentley, A. (1966). *Musical Ability in Children and its Measurement.* London: Harrap.

A journal article:
> Cox, G. (1990). The Legacy of Folk Song: the Influence of Cecil Sharp on Music Education. *British Journal of Music Education,* 7(2), 89–97.

A chapter in another author's book
> Rainbow, B. (1988). The Land With Music: Reality and Myth in Music Education. In Anthony Kemp (ed.), *Research in Music Education: A Festschrift for Arnold Bentley.* Reading: International Society for Music Education.

Note that the titles of books and journals are identified by using italics as above, or, if the article is being typed, by underlining. References are assembled in alphabetical order of authors' family names; where two authors bearing the same name feature in the list be guided by the initials as in any telephone directory. Works, within authors, are listed in chronological order of publication; in those instances where more than one work by an author bears the same date ascribe an 'a' and 'b' (see page 136) and ensure that these also appear in the text . For further details of referencing the reader is encouraged to consult the *Publication Manual of the American Psychological Association* (1984).

Other Aspects of Research Reporting

In addition to offering advice on how the main headings of a research report are used it is important that this chapter should offer help in terms of additional questions which frequently arise in research reporting. Some of these relate to:

Tables and Figures

Tables and figures should be separately numbered to facilitate cross-referencing with the text. Each requires a title or caption which should state explicitly what information is being presented. Tables comprise statistical information which can be typed or word processed whereas figures are non-statistical and may take the form of graphs, drawings, and photographs supplied by the author. Where ever possible figures and tables should not exceed one page. In instances where the report will be published it is important to ensure that figures are of good quality; the publisher will normally expect material to be in black and white.

Tables and figures do not merely duplicate what is presented within the text. If well constructed they will present the information in a much more accessible, concise and clear form. All figures and tables should be referred to in the text, the author being required only to highlight the main points presented in each.

Constructing effective tables can be a fairly complex process and the reader is referred again to the *Publication Manual of the American Psychological Association* or to any of the principal journals in the field. Briefly, all rows and columns require subheadings and the use of lines should be minimized and restricted to horizontal only; there is no need to box tables. Table 1 shows these points clearly.

Table 1 *Example of title and heading for a table containing results*

Table 0 Means and standard deviations of fifth grade students on academic measures

Measure	Experimental group 1		Experimental group 2		Control group	
	Mean	Standard deviation	Mean	Standard deviation	Mean	Standard deviation
Reading						
Arithmetic						
Spelling						
Science						
Social Studies						

(From Wierzma, 1986, p. 291)

If the article is to be sent for publication in a journal assemble the tables and figures on individual pages separately at the end of the script. Within the text indicate the most desired position for the table or figure in the following way:

Table 1 about here

Remember that the type-setter may not be able to place it in this exact position due to page-breaks. If the article is for presentation at a seminar or a conference the organizers may require a different procedure for the placement of tables and figures; it is important to consult the instructions provided in the call for papers.

Quotations

As already indicated it is important that authors indicate very clearly the division between what is their own text

151

and that which has been drawn directly from the literature. The styles for doing this may slightly differ from one journal to another; some use single quotation marks, other use double. Most journals make a distinction between long and short quotations, the dividing line frequently being drawn at about 40 words. Short quotations may be placed within the body of the script and identified with quotation marks; those which are longer than this can be typed single spaced and indented. For example, the *Publication Manual of the American Psychological Association* (1984) states

> Use three ellipsis points (...) within a sentence to indicate that you have omitted material from the original source....Use four points to indicate any omission between two sentences (literally a period followed by three spaced dots....). Do not use ellipsis points at the beginning or end of any quotation unless, in order to prevent misinterpretation, you need to emphasize that the quotation begins or ends in midsentence. (p. 70)

As in the above example, make sure that the reference, including the page number, is shown; this applies to all quotations, however short. Frequently, journals type-set block quotations in smaller type as above; if this facility is available on the word processor make use of it. Several journals dispense with quotation marks at the beginnings and ends of block quotations; however, they are used for quotations within quotations. Case studies, action research and other forms of qualitative research often make use of passages drawn directly from interviews; these may be dealt with in the same kind of fashion.

The general advice, often given, is to be sparing in the use of quotations from the literature. Unless a quotation is totally 'on target', in terms of the point that is being made, it may be more effective to make a paraphrase. Very occasionally a quotation is discovered which makes a central point far more eloquently than the author can; in such an instance it would be unwise to attempt a paraphrase.

Appendices

Appendices are more frequently used in theses than in conference papers or articles. They are particularly useful when significant information such as a test or question-naire, a computer program, or a piece of apparatus has been specially designed for the purpose of the research. Alternatively, in historical research, appendices are used to reproduce unpublished documents, such as letters, which are central to the research in question. The general rule to adopt is, that if the material is absolutely essential for a reader to be able to replicate the work, and if by including it in the body of the text it would break the flow, then it should be included as an appendix.

Appendices should be numbered, supplied with titles, cross-referenced in the text, and placed after the references.

Notes and Footnotes

Some methodologies make more use of notes or footnotes than others. Some journals explicitly discourage their use maintaining that any information worthy of note should be integrated within the body of the text. Where these methods are used all footnotes are numbered and refer-enced with the use of these numbers in the text. The notes themselves are assembled in numerical order at the end of the article immediately before the references. (An example of this can be seen in Chapter 4 on pages 84 and 85 and also in Koza, 1990; and Gordon, 1991.) In some theses and papers footnotes are placed at the bottom of the relevant page. Sometimes, in historical research, referencing is carried out using both these methods.

Abstracts

Conference and seminar programmes sometimes require abstracts and most journals do also. For example, the *International Journal of Music Education* publishes abstracts in French, German and Spanish for all its articles thus considerably widening the readership. The abstract is a brief, free-standing document and may be the only part of the report that someone undertaking a search will read. It is restricted to concise sentences which describe the topic, the procedure, the findings and the conclusions without going into any of the finer details. The abstract must be accurate and brief, rarely exceeding 200 words.

Anonymity of Subjects

Utmost confidentiality must be maintained for all those persons who have been tested, observed, interviewed or questioned during the collection of the data. In testing groups this presents little problem, but in case studies, pseudonyms should replace real names. The use of pseudonyms may help retain the atmosphere of individuality which is lost if cases are given numbers or letter names.

The use of photographs to provide more graphic information about, say, the testing situation, may also unwittingly disclose the identity of a student. In these instances facial features should be blocked out. With the increasing use of video recording in research procedures and in the preparation of theses a similar problem can occur. More recent technology now allows for facial characteristics to be obscured electronically in video recordings.

Sexist Language

Increasingly the adoption of non-sexist language in research reporting is required in order to avoid sex bias and discrimination. At first this can create severe problems for authors until they have developed the techniques to evade the problem. For example, a sentence like 'a pupil has the ability to evaluate his own compositions' can be adapted by the sparing use of 'his or her' but not 'its'. Another method frequently used in circumstances where it does not alter the sense is to adopt the plural: 'pupils have the ability to evaluate their own compositions'. In some situations the sentence can be re-phrased thus: 'the ability to evaluate compositions is often displayed by the pupil'. Similarly terms such as 'mankind', 'manpower' and increasingly 'chairman' are being replaced by the use of 'people', 'personnel' and 'chairperson'.

Final Comments

When the first draft is complete it is important to undertake a thorough check for mis-spellings, grammatical errors and imprecise language. The first can be dealt with by using a word processing spelling check, but bear in mind that this does not identify misused words. Be prepared to rewrite passages completely where it is felt that the precise meaning remains obscure or in instances where space can be saved by adopting sharper language. Always ask other colleagues to read final drafts simply because a fresh pair of eyes will often identify errors and obscurities which have been overlooked however many times they have been checked. Particularly check that all references have been listed, that they are complete and fully accurate.

Finally, good research reporting becomes second nature to those who spend time reading the most prestigious research journals. When unsure about a particular procedure be prepared to be guided by a journal which is refereed and which has an international reputation.

References

American Psychological Association (1984). *Publication Manual of the American Psychological Association* (3rd edn.). Washington, DC: APA.

Bartle, G. (1986). Music Education in the Soviet Union. *International Journal of Music Education*, 8, 33–37.

Bartle, G. (1988). The Grass on the Other Side of the Fence...Two Contrasting Models for the Organization of Music Education for the Beginner Performer. In J. Dobbs (ed.), *International Music Education: ISME Yearbook*, XV, 196–202.

Brand, M. (1984). Music Teachers Versus Researchers: A Truce. *Council of Research in Music Education Bulletin*, 80, 1–13.

Bergee, M. J. (1992). The Relationship between Music Education Majors' Personality Profiles, Other Education Majors' Profiles, and Selected Indicators of Music Teaching Success. *Council for Research in Music Education Bulletin*, 112, 5–15.

Cox, G. (1990). The Legacy of Folk Song: The Influence of Cecil Sharp on Music Education. *British Journal of Music Education*, 7 (2), 89–97.

Cox, G. (1992). 'The Right Place of Music in Education': A History of Musical Education in England 1872–1928 with Special Reference to the Role of HMI. Unpublished PhD. Thesis, University of Reading.

Crowther, R., Durkin, K., Shire, B. and Hargreaves, D. J. (1985). Influences on the Development of Children's Conservation-type Responses to Music. *Council for Research in Music Education Bulletin*, 85, 26–37.

Davies, C. (1992). Listen to my Song: A Study of Songs Invented by Children Aged 5 to 7 Years. *British Journal of Music Education*, 9 (1), 19–48.

Fiske, H. E. (1985). Cognition Strategies in Music Listening. *Council for Research in Music Education Bulletin*, 85, 56–75.

Gordon, E. E. (1991). A Study of the Characteristics of the Instrument Timbre Preference Test. *Council for Research in Music Education Bulletin*, 110, 33–51.

Hassler, M. (1989). Musical Talent and Musical Spatial Ability. *Canadian Music Educator (Special Supplement)*, 30 (2), 39–45.

Hassler, M., Birbaumer, N. and Feil, A. (1987). Musical Talent and Visual-Spatial Ability: Onset of Puberty. *Psychology of Music*, 15, 141–151.

Kemp, A. E. (1985). Psychological Androgyny in Musicians. *Council for Research in Music Education Bulletin*, 85, 102–108.

Kemp, A. E. (1987). Research in Music Education and the Teacher. *Council for Research in Music Education Bulletin*, 91, 1–2.

Kemp, A. E. (ed.) (1988). *Research in Music Education: A Festschrift for Arnold Bentley.* Reading: International Society for Music Education.

Koza, J. E. (1990). Music Instruction in the Nineteenth Century: Views from *Godey's Lady's Book*, 1830–77. *Journal of Research in Music Education*, 38 (4), 245–257.

Kwami, R. (1991). An Approach to the Use of West African Musics in the Classroom based on Age and Gender Classifications. *British Journal of Music Education*, 8 (2), 119–137.

Lephard, L. (ed.) (1985). The Education of Exceptionally Gifted Children. *International Journal of Music Education*, 6, 39–58.

Lephard, L. (ed.) (1986). Bi-Cultural Music Education. *International Journal of Music Education*, 7, 23–39.

Lephard, L. (1988). *Music Education in International Perspective: The People's Republic of China.* Darling Heights, Queensland: Music International.

Nagel, J. J., Himle, D. P. and Papsdorf, J. D. (1989). Cognitive-Behavioural Treatment of Musical Performance Anxiety. *Psychology of Music*, 17, 12–21.

Okafor, R. C. (1991). Music in Nigerian Education. *Journal of Research in Music Education*, 108, 59–68.

Paynter, J. (ed.) (1987). Music Education in Nordic Countries. *British Journal of Music Education*, 4 (3), 251–252.

Rainbow, B. (1967). *The Land without Music*. London: Novello.

Rainbow, B. (1970). *The Choral Revival in the Anglican Church 1839–1872.* London: Barrie & Jenkins.

Rainbow, B. (1991). *Music in Educational Thought and Practice.* Aberystwyth: Boethius.

Scott, C. R. (1990). Closing the Gap Between Research and Practice. In Jack P. B. Dobbs (ed.), *Music Education: Facing the Future.* Christchurch, NZ: International Society for Music Education.

Sloboda, J. A. and Howe, M. J. A. (1991). Biographical Precursors of Musical Excellence: An Interview Study. *Psychology of Music*, 19, 3–21.

Southcott, J. (1990). A Music Education Pioneer – Dr Satis Naronna Barton Coleman. *British Journal of Music Education*, 7 (2), 123–132.

Standley, J. M. and Madsen, C. K. (1991). An Observation Procedure to Differentiate Teaching Experience and Expertise in Music Education. *Journal of Research in Music Education,* 39 (1), 5–11.

Swanwick, K. (1991). Musical Criticism and Musical Development. *British Journal of Music Education,* 8 (2), 139–148.

Swanwick, K. and Tillman, J. (1986). The Sequence of Musical Development. *British Journal of Music Education,* 3 (3), 305–339.

Taebel, D. K. (1990). An Assessment of the Classroom Performance of Music Teachers. *Journal of Research in Music Education,* 38 (1), 5–23.

Verney, J. P. (1991). The Integrated Instrumental Teacher: Learning to Play Through Performance, Listening and Composition. *British Journal of Music Education,* 8 (3), 245–269.

Welch. G. F. (1985). Variability of Practice and Knowledge of Results as Factors in Learning to Sing in Tune. *Council for Research in Music Education Bulletin,* 85, 238–247.

Wierzma,W. (1986). *Research Methods in Education* (4th edn.). Newton, MA: Allyn and Bacon.